ART

from the

SWAMP

ART

from the

SWAMP

How Washington Bureaucrats
Squander Millions on Awful Art

BRUCE COLE

Encounter Books
New York • London

First American edition published in 2018 by Encounter Books,
an activity of Encounter for Culture and Education, Inc.,
a nonprofit, tax exempt corporation.
Encounter Books website address: www.encounterbooks.com

Manufactured in the United States and printed on
acid-free paper. The paper used in this publication meets
the minimum requirements of ANSI/NISO Z39.48–1992
(R 1997) (*Permanence of Paper*).

Image credits:
1.3a & 1.3b: Images courtesy of the Eisenhower Memorial Commission;
Memorial Design by Gehry Partners, LLP; Tapestry Design by Tomas Osinski;
Sculpture by Sergey Eylanbekov.
1.4, 4.1, 4.2: Created by B. Cole and J. Studemeyer.
All other images are in the public domain.

FIRST AMERICAN EDITION

LIBRARY OF CONGRESS CATALOGING-IN-PUBLICATION DATA
Names: Cole, Bruce, 1938– author.
Title: Art from the swamp : how Washington bureaucrats
squander millions on awful art / by Bruce Cole.
Description: New York : Encounter Books, 2018. |
Includes bibliographical references and index.
Identifiers: LCCN 2018010777 (print) | LCCN 2018016433 (ebook) |
ISBN 9781594039973 (ebook) | ISBN 9781594039966 (hardcover : alk. paper)
Subjects: LCSH: Federal aid to the arts—United States. |
Waste in government spending—United States.
Classification: LCC N8837 (ebook) | LCC N8837 .C65 2018 (print) |
DDC 701/.03—dc23
LC record available at https://lccn.loc.gov/2018010777

Interior page design and composition: BooksByBruce.com

For my family

Special thanks to:

The Staff and Fellows at EPPC
The Achelis and Bodman Foundation
The Bradley Foundation
Michael Bekesha at Judicial Watch
Leslie Lenkowsky
J. Bradley Studemeyer

Contents

Foreword

by

Roger Kimball

This is one foreword that I wish I did not have to write.

When my friend Bruce Cole died suddenly in January 2018, age 79, he left the manuscript of this book about Washington's patronage of the arts almost complete. In a world in which the operations of Clotho, Lachesis, and Atropos—the three Fates who spin, measure out, and finally snip the skein of life—were not so preemptory, it would have been Bruce himself who would have offered these few stage-setting words.

But it was not to be. Bruce, a historian of Renaissance art and of American civics, was also the longest-serving director of the National Endowment for the Humanities, a post he held from 2001 to 2009. He was also the author of fourteen books on various aspects of Renaissance art, American civic literacy, and related topics. In 2008, President George W. Bush awarded him the Presidential Citizens Medal "for his work to strengthen our national memory and ensure that our country's heritage is passed on to future generations." The preservation of national memory and the preservation of our heritage were abiding leitmotifs in Bruce's career, both in his voluminous writing and in his many administrative activities.

Bruce's last official perch was as a scholar at the Ethics and

Public Policy Center in Washington, D.C. He was a potent com-
mentator on a clutch of public controversies, weighing in most
recently on the heated debate over the proposed Dwight D.
Eisenhower Memorial in Washington, a controversy that looms
large in this book.

The title *Art from the Swamp* suggests the spongey and envel-
oping nature of the phenomenon Bruce seeks to anatomize in
this book. For what started in 1783 with an unrealized public
commission by the Confederation Congress for an equestrian
statue of George Washington has ballooned, like every bureaucracy that pulsates in the pullulating ground of Washington, into
a sprawling and expensive congeries of programs, initiatives,
grants, set-asides, commissions, and mandatory spending requirements overseen by the General Services Administration's Art in
Architecture Program, the National Endowment for the Arts,
and other swampy entities. The result, as Bruce catalogues in the
following pages, is a corrupt process that disgorges a panoply of
art and architecture at taxpayer expense but most often without
regard to taxpayer taste or preference. Bruce shows just how vast
the empire of government patronage has become in an Appendix
which lists every known work of government funded art and
architecture from 1975 to 2016. It is a long list.

I said that when Bruce died the manuscript for this book was
almost complete. I have to emphasize the adverb: almost. Without
the tireless and expert intervention of Bruce's longtime assistant
and EPPC colleague J. Bradley Studemeyer, *Art from the Swamp*
would have remained a work *in potentia*. It was he who dotted the
I's and crossed the T's, filled in the lacunae, polished the rough
edges, supplied the missing quotations, and checked and doubled
the many sources that Bruce consulted in writing this book. Mr.
Studemeyer's work was the indispensable coping stone. I am grate-
ful to have this opportunity to thank him for his labors.

Introduction

Washington bureaucrats spend millions of dollars each year on artwork and do so without the knowledge or consent of most of the taxpayers who foot the bill. Commissioned by a labyrinthine thicket of unelected commissions, committees, boards, and panels, this government art is unwanted, unloved, and astronomically expensive. This book will explore, and often expose, how federal funds are used to produce awful art through an examination of the Eisenhower Memorial on the National Mall in Washington, D.C., the General Services Administration's Art in Architecture Program, and the National Endowment for the Arts.

The history of government-sponsored art is a long one. For millennia, public works of art and architecture have been commissioned, and paid for, by rulers. From ancient Egypt to our time, paintings, sculptures, monuments, memorials, and buildings furthered the aims of emperors, kings, popes, and dictators, among others. Pyramids, pagan temples, soaring cathedrals, and untold numbers of paintings, mosaics, and statues tell us as much about the character of those who made them as do words in books and manuscripts.

Our relationship with art and architecture is not merely a one-way street; as Winston Churchill said, "We shape our buildings, and afterwards our buildings shape us." Sometimes such shaping is evil, as with Albert Speer's crushing designs for Hitler's Berlin, and sometimes it is good, as with the Lincoln Memorial on the National Mall in Washington. This is also true of paintings and sculptures.

This book is about public art commissioned by the government of the United States, a country that has been commissioning works of art for almost as long as it has been independent. In 1783, the year the Revolutionary War ended and five years before the ratification of the Constitution, an equestrian statue of George Washington was commissioned by the Confederation Congress. Although the statue was never created, a precedent was set for federal patronage of art and architecture. The following year, the Virginia General Assembly also commissioned a statue of Washington (which was sculpted by Jean-Antoine Houdon between 1785 and 1791), an early example of state sponsorship of art.[1]

After Congress held its first session in the District of Columbia in 1800, funds were appropriated for the Capitol, its decoration, and for other federal buildings in the capital city and beyond. For the rest of the nineteenth century and through the early twentieth century, however, art commissions were sporadic and unsystematic.

With the vast expansion of the machinery of the state during Franklin Roosevelt's presidential terms, Washington's role as art patron expanded considerably. Beginning at the height of the Great Depression in 1933 and lasting until 1943, a series of government schemes employed out-of-work artists to create new works. The first of these, the Public Works of Art Project, put hundreds of artists on the federal payroll. When the Public Works of Art Project met its demise six months after its founding, the Treasury Section of Painting and Sculpture (later the Section of Fine Arts) rose to take its place.

Under this program, artists competed for commissions for new public buildings, including post offices, schools, museums, libraries, and embassies. While the Section of Painting and Sculpture covered works for new federal buildings, the Treasury Relief Art Project paid artists for works to be placed within preexisting federal structures. It was the Works Progress Administration's Federal Art Project, however, that commissioned the most artists, some 5,000 of whom were responsible for creating more than 225,000 works,[2] all of which became the property of the US government.

The subjects of New Deal artworks varied. Some of them, especially those in post offices and other federal buildings, depicted events from local history; others pictured industry and technology. Many, however, depicted ordinary men and women struggling through the Great Depression.

The New Deal art programs employed traditionally minded figurative artists, but also gave work to many artists with progressive (even radical) views who later developed more abstract styles. A few future stars were subsidized (Jackson Pollock and Mark Rothko, for example), but the vast majority of New Deal artists made little impact on the history of American art and today many of their works remain unknown.

With the onset of the Second World War, funding priorities in the federal government shifted. By the end of 1943, all of the New Deal–era art programs had folded. In 1949 a new federal agency, the General Services Administration (GSA), was founded to consolidate various federal management programs. This agency will figure large throughout this book, because though it was created to manage federal properties and serve federal agencies, it revived the practice of federal art patronage in 1963; with some interruptions, it has been commissioning new artwork ever since.

This agency now houses the Art in Architecture program, a successor to New Deal–era patronage that is responsible for spending millions of dollars on art each year for new and restored federal buildings. GSA, along with a host of other federal agencies, also plays an important role in the construction of memorials and monuments on the National Mall in Washington, D.C. The Eisenhower Memorial, the newest addition to the National Mall, is the subject of the first chapter to follow. The twists, turns, and mountains of taxpayer dollars expended to begin construction serve as good an introduction as any to the art made by the Swamp.

—Bruce Cole

The Eisenhower Memorial

Submerged among funding for proving grounds, military personnel, and armor in the Department of Defense Appropriations Act, 2000, is a series of short paragraphs authorizing a memorial to Dwight David Eisenhower, the thirty-fourth president of the United States, a federal commission to oversee its construction, and $300,000 to "remain available [to the Commission] until expended."[1] This legislation, and its ramifications over time, serves as an object lesson of how a small group of powerful people decided on, legislated for, and ultimately created a memorial that almost no one wanted. That single innocuous appropriation for a few hundred thousand dollars grew, over almost two decades, into public expenditures well in excess of $100 million for a single pet project. Compared to other items in the national budget, the money spent on this memorial is but decimal dust, but as an example of how the Washington Swamp creates art and architecture, there can be few finer examples.

It is, in truth, highly unusual for presidents of the United States to be memorialized on the National Mall. Most presidents, following the lead of George Washington, return to their home states after the completion of their terms and are thus usually memorialized there. This memorialization can take the form of a simple monument or, in a more recent trend, an official presidential library, such as Eisenhower's in Abilene, Kansas, where the former presidents are buried and their papers are stored.

There are, however, a few exceptions to this tradition, starting with a monument, begun in 1848 but not completed until 1888, honoring George Washington. Subsequent memorials were built on or near the Mall to honor James A. Garfield (1887), Abraham Lincoln (1922), Ulysses S. Grant (1922), Thomas Jefferson (1943), and Franklin Delano Roosevelt (1997). Each of these memorializes a president who was, without a doubt, transformational in the country's history: Washington, the first president; Jefferson, author of the Declaration of Independence; Lincoln, the Great Emancipator; Grant, the general who reunited the country; Garfield, the first president to be assassinated; and Franklin Roosevelt, our longest-serving president. Each of the presidents memorialized shaped the course of the nation in unprecedented and permanent ways.

The case for Eisenhower is not as strong. His role as supreme commander of the Allied Expeditionary Forces in Europe was undoubtedly a great achievement, but his victory over Nazi Germany did not mark the end of the Second World War, which raged on in the Pacific theater for months. Surely figures such as Gen. Douglas MacArthur or Adm. Chester Nimitz played roles as important as Eisenhower's in bringing the War to an end, yet none of the other military leaders has a memorial on the National Mall. Rather, all are honored on the Mall by the gigantic National World War II Memorial.

During his two terms as president, Eisenhower ended the Korean War, kept the peace with the Soviet Union, and made some progress in enforcing civil rights in the South. None of these accomplishments could be deemed trivial, but one might ask if his presidency was as crucial as that of his predecessor Harry Truman. It was Truman, after all, who oversaw the victory over

Japan, yet there is no monument to Truman on the Mall. What about Ulysses S. Grant, the general who defeated the Confederacy during the Civil War and saved the Union? The bronze and marble monument to Grant at the foot of Capitol Hill memorializes him as a *general*, not as a two-term president; the monument is covered with depictions of infantry, artillery, and cavalry.

Before the enabling legislation for the Eisenhower Memorial was introduced in the Department of Defense Appropriations Act, 2000, there had been no national movement for a memorial to Eisenhower on the Mall. Perhaps this was because fitting tributes to Eisenhower already existed elsewhere. The aforementioned Eisenhower Presidential Library and Museum in Abilene had been open for decades, the Old Executive Office Building in downtown Washington was renamed the Eisenhower Executive Building in 1999, and in 2004 the enormous National World War II Memorial was opened on the Mall to honor all who served in the conflict.

So, one might ask, absent a groundswell for a memorial to Eisenhower decades after his presidency, and with several memorials to him already in place, how was it possible that legislation authorizing its construction was passed through Congress? The answer begins with two influential senators and a former aide to President Eisenhower.

Sen. Ted Stevens (R.-Alaska) and Sen. Daniel Inouye (D.-Hawaii) both served with distinction in World War II. Stevens was an Army Air Forces transport pilot who "flew the Hump" in the China-Burma-India theater; Inouye fought as part of the famed 442nd Infantry Regiment, with whom he earned the Medal of Honor. These two men, along with Rocco Siciliano, a fellow veteran who served in the Eisenhower administration from 1953 to 1959 and later became an influential lawyer in the Los Angeles area, decided that Eisenhower needed a memorial. This memorial was not to be just any memorial, but a grand one indeed.

The founding legislation for the Eisenhower Memorial

Commission called for the establishment of a twelve-member bipartisan commission composed of four members of the Senate, four members of the House of Representatives, and four presidential appointees. The original members of the Commission were Rocco Siciliano (made chairman at the first meeting in April 2001), Sen. Daniel Inouye, Sen. Ted Stevens, Sen. Pat Roberts, Sen. Jack Reed, Rep. Jerry Moran, Rep. Mac Thornberry, Rep. Dennis Moore, Rep. Leonard Boswell, Alfred Geduldig, Susan Harris, and David Eisenhower. The presence of a member of the Eisenhower family on the Commission came as no surprise. As the fifteen-year saga to arrive at a suitable design for the Franklin D. Roosevelt Memorial had shown, the opinions of family can make or break memorial efforts. Senator Inouye, in particular, spoke frequently of the need to include the family in the memorial process and garner their approval for the memorial.

Siciliano, it seems, had reason to believe that family opposition would not be an issue, because by the time the Commission was established, Siciliano had worked with the Eisenhower family for decades. In addition to working in the Eisenhower administration, he had served a lengthy spell as the chairman of the Eisenhower World Affairs Institute (EWAI), a Washington-based policy center. The founding director and first president of the EWAI was Susan Eisenhower, one of the president's granddaughters. In 2000, the EWAI merged with Gettysburg College's Center for Political and Strategic Studies and became known as the Eisenhower Institute, with Susan Eisenhower serving as its president and chief executive officer.

Although it was Susan's brother, David (after whom the country retreat for sitting presidents, Camp David, is named), who was appointed by President Clinton to be a member of the Eisenhower Memorial Commission, Susan and her sister Anne frequently attended meetings, and their comments recorded in the meeting minutes far outnumber those made by David. The relationships between Siciliano and the Eisenhowers, especially Susan

Eisenhower, came to have an enormous impact on the development of the Memorial.

For the first few *years* of its existence, the Commission was, amazingly, uncertain about what the Eisenhower Memorial would be—a sort of study center or think tank like the Woodrow Wilson Center (described as a "living" memorial), a bricks-and-mortar memorial, or something else entirely? Even before the nature of the memorial had been established, though, Senator Roberts lobbied for Kansas as the memorial site, saying that the Kansas delegation was interested in Abilene as its location. He also noted that the Old Executive Office Building had been renamed the Eisenhower Executive Office Building, a comment that seems to imply that there was already an appropriate memorial to the president in Washington. Senator Stevens, on the other hand, suggested that the memorial be a "notable attraction" situated "across the Potomac," noting that although the Mall was a "preeminent location," it came with issues that might "prolong the project," a prescient statement indeed.[2]

In 2002 the responsibility for the development of a memorial concept was turned over to a Legacy Committee, headed by Johns Hopkins University professor Louis Galambos, the coeditor of *The Papers of Dwight David Eisenhower*. Professor Galambos explained to the Commission that his job was to "extract the essence of Eisenhower's lasting legacy, and to present it in non-technical terms to the general public and to scholars."[3] It was the matter of enshrining this "lasting legacy" that would become the chief issue for the Commission: while several of the members (including Siciliano and Stevens) appeared to lean toward a physical memorial from the very beginning, Susan Eisenhower made it clear, from some of the earliest meetings, that her preference was for a living memorial.

Susan Eisenhower first introduced a proposal for a living memorial at a meeting in February 2002, and she noted explicitly that the plan was being introduced on behalf of "the various organizations founded by or named for her grandfather" rather than the Eisenhower family (her sister Anne, she said, spoke "on behalf of the family").[4] In March 2004, the Eisenhower Memorial Commission agreed to provide a nine-month planning grant to the Eisenhower Institute to examine the feasibility of the various Eisenhower legacy organizations working together on a living memorial under its direction. For this work, Susan Eisenhower's organization was paid the princely sum of $400,000, though she was quick to point out to the Commission that "she would receive no personal compensation for this effort, adding that her personal interest was to provide the kind of leadership that would ensure the family's continued support for the Eisenhower Memorial."[5]

The issue of personal interest, though, does not end with matters of compensation. The narrative that Susan Eisenhower introduced at the meeting in February 2002, that of a clear separation between legacy organizations and the Eisenhower family, is muddied by her comments at the June 2003 meeting, as she is quoted as saying, "*the Eisenhower family* wished to elevate the Eisenhower Institute into a paramount Eisenhower [i]nstitution for the purpose of leading and coordinating the other Eisenhower organizations"[6] [emphasis mine]. At the end of the meeting, she asked again about "who would have the authority to lead discussions among the Eisenhower organizations," seemingly angling for recognition as that authority. The barriers separating the Eisenhower legacy organizations from the Eisenhower family, then, look much more permeable than Susan let on in her first comments to the Commission.

Susan Eisenhower's outsized role in the memorial process appears to have led to some tension between her and Siciliano. For example, at the end of the June 2003 meeting of the Eisenhower Memorial Commission, Senator Inouye responded to Susan's question regarding the authority to lead discussions among Eisenhower legacy organizations by saying not only that she had been "selected" for that role, but that "this was the reason for her presence as a member of the Commission."[7] Siciliano immediately interjected, reminding the members in attendance that she was, in fact, not a commissioner, but that her brother, David, was the family's representative on the Commission. Inouye then asked for the record to be corrected to show that he "regarded Susan Eisenhower as a spokesperson on this occasion for David Eisenhower." His first comment, however, suggests that Susan was perceived, even by members of the Commission, as wielding considerable influence over the Commission's work.

As it turns out, Susan Eisenhower's securing of the $400,000 grant from the Commission was her last substantial act as director of the Eisenhower Institute. In 2012 she testified before Congress about the decision to leave that position, stating in her written testimony, "In my role, I helped obtain a grant from the Eisenhower Memorial Commission to the Eisenhower Institute for the purposes of fleshing out the details of what this living memorial component might look like. On securing the grant, I stepped down from my position at the Institute to assure that there would be no suggestion that I was personally benefitting in any way from the grant."[8] Exactly what happened to make her think such a step was necessary, especially after her comments to the Commission that indicated that she wanted the proposal to be developed "under her leadership,"[9] is unknown.

The Commission's FY 2015 budget justification summarizes what eventually happened to the proposal for a living memorial, noting that the proposal "fell short of its initial aim, as representatives of several Eisenhower Legacy Organizations were unable to agree on a cooperative mode for a 'Living Memorial.' In June of 2007, representatives of Eisenhower Legacy Organizations (ELO), including Susan Eisenhower, ultimately agreed that 'a full consensus was achieved among attendees that the *Legacy Organizations are the Living Memorial to Dwight David Eisenhower*' [emphasis in original]."[10]

Because the various legacy organizations could not achieve consensus on a model for the "living memorial," the idea was jettisoned, though the budget justification describes the end result in somewhat amiable terms, with "a full consensus" achieved on the idea that a living memorial would be redundant. The $400,000 grant to Susan Eisenhower's Eisenhower Institute apparently proved only that the various Eisenhower legacy groups could not agree on a single plan or come to a mutual compromise on what the memorial should be.

In the testimony she submitted to Congress, however, Susan Eisenhower recalled the outcome of discussions regarding a living memorial very differently. She disputed the claim that the plan for a living memorial fell apart due to legacy organization infighting, writing, "The Eisenhower Memorial Commission (EMC) staff, and perhaps the commission's chairman, reviewed the study and apparently decided to reject the ELO proposal. The EMC gave little if no encouragement to the legacy organizations to reconfigure their proposal—in fact a number of developments between the ELOs and the EMC staff led to an eventual collapse of this process . . . For the last several years there has been virtually no contact between the Eisenhower Memorial Commission staff and the ELOs. In fact considerable friction has occurred because the EMC staff has been using the legacy organization's contacts for their own purposes. The atmosphere between the two groups is very negative."[11] Perhaps anticipating that Commission members would dispute her narrative (on the issue of a living memorial and on other aspects of the project), Susan added, "The minutes of the Eisenhower Memorial Commission are often misleading with respect to our family's position, through the drafter's choice of words."

Even before Susan Eisenhower submitted a proposal for a living memorial, however, one important name had already been recorded in the meeting minutes: that of Frank Gehry. Years before the Commission made any definitive choice between a physical memorial and a living memorial, let alone discussed the form a physical memorial might take, chairman Rocco Siciliano had mentioned the "starchitect" Frank Gehry in a meeting.

On April 26, 2001, at the second recorded meeting of the Eisenhower Memorial Commission (though the first in which any substantive discussion occurred), Siciliano expressed "his thoughts about the kind of architect represented by Frank Gehry."[12] This unsubtle name-dropping comes out of nowhere in the meeting minutes; neither the comments before nor after have anything to do with designs or designers. He also brought up Gehry in 2005, mentioning the need to hire an architect "of Gehry's stature," and again in 2006, saying that Gehry had "indicated an interest in a possible design of the Eisenhower Memorial."[13]

By the time the Eisenhower Memorial Commission came into being, Gehry and Siciliano already had a long history together, one that dated back to the early 1980s. Siciliano was a founding member of the board of the Museum of Contemporary Art, Los Angeles, and served on that board when it awarded Gehry, then relatively unknown, one of his first important commissions. Siciliano was also on the board of Los Angeles Philharmonic when Gehry received the contract to design its new home, the Walt Disney Concert Hall, though Siciliano has stated "for the record" that he played no part in helping Gehry receive that particular commission.[14]

Siciliano's prior dealings with Gehry have led critics of the memorial to suggest that Siciliano, from almost the very beginning of the process, had Gehry in mind for the Eisenhower Memorial architect and then put his thumb on the scale to ensure his hiring. Indeed, in the Eisenhower Memorial Commission meeting minutes from before the search for an architect was officially under way, the same period of time in which Siciliano is recorded as bringing Gehry up on three separate occasions, the name of only one other architect, Richard Meier (designer of the Getty Center in Los Angeles, where Siciliano was a trustee from 1982 to 1995),[15]

FIGURE 1.1   WALT DISNEY CONCERT HALL

Source: Carol M. Highsmith Archive, Library of Congress, Prints & Photographs Division

Modernist architect Frank Gehry's Walt Disney Concert Hall, Los Angeles, California

appears in the meeting minutes, and he was mentioned only in passing.

In the early 2000s, when the Commission was beginning to contemplate designers, Gehry was the architect of the moment. His enthusiastic (and, by necessity, extremely wealthy) patrons employed him to design their museums, corporate headquarters, university buildings, and condos. From his Guggenheim Museum in Bilbao, Spain, to Los Angeles's Disney Concert Hall to "New York by Gehry," a New York City residential high rise, to the Fondation Louis Vuitton in Paris, his designs are trademarks, not only for the architect, but also for those who employ him seeking the prestige and prominence his buildings confer.

The process leading up to Gehry's selection as architect was unorthodox and therefore controversial. Historically the process for choosing designers for memorials or sculptures on the National

Mall has been through an open competition in which design proposals are submitted. The White House and the Washington Monument were both built after such competitions. This time-honored approach has been used for centuries because it encourages applications from a wide range of entrants with diverse ideas and viewpoints. It is the most open, fair, and democratic way to select a designer for a memorial.

An open competition was, for example, used to select the design for the Vietnam Veterans Memorial. More than 2,500 designers registered for the competition, and more than 1,400 designs were submitted and displayed for public inspection at Andrews Air Force Base. To ensure that it was a truly blind contest, each design proposal was identified by a number rather than the author's name. Some two hundred entries survived the first cut. A second cull reduced the number to thirty-nine. After deliberations, a jury selected proposal 1026, submitted by Maya Lin, a hitherto-unknown student at Yale University.

One hundred and one designs were submitted for the statue in the Jefferson Memorial,[16] nearly six hundred for the Franklin D. Roosevelt Memorial (though the chosen "winner" was never built after public outcry over the design),[17] more than four hundred for the National World War II Memorial.[18] More than nine hundred entries were submitted for the Martin Luther King Jr. Memorial.[19] In 2015, a blind competition for designs for the World War I Memorial, just off the National Mall, was launched, open to anyone older than eighteen years from any country, and it received 350 entries.[20]

Despite considerable precedent, both in this country and internationally, this equitable, time-tested process was rejected by the Eisenhower Memorial Commission under Rocco Siciliano's chairmanship. Instead, the Commission chose to use a variation of GSA's postmodernist Design Excellence program, which allows only licensed architectural firms to submit their portfolios (*not* design concepts) for consideration.[21]

Curiously enough, the Commission seemed set on receiving a certain kind of portfolio even before it had put out an official request for portfolios. The Pre-Design Program that the Commission put out "communicated to the designer what the National Eisenhower Memorial should be, including goals, requirements, constraints, and opportunities."[22] Among the goals and requirements, the Pre-Design Program called for a "new vision of memorialization: a new paradigm for memorials."[23] This is hardly language that suggests that any traditionally minded firm would have a chance, but exactly the sort of language that would appeal to a designer like Frank Gehry.

Although the competition was, in a strict sense, "open," the Eisenhower Memorial Commission did not simply wait to see which firms would notice the project announcement during the fifty-five days it appeared on FedBizOpps, the federal contract–posting website. Instead, as Eisenhower Memorial Commission Executive Director Carl Reddel admitted in his written testimony to Congress in 2012, "After the RFQ was published in FedBizOpps and published on other sites as noted previously, with the approval of the GSA Contracting Officer, letters were sent by the Eisenhower Memorial Commission Executive Architect to thirty architects and landscape architects announcing the RFQ for design services for the Eisenhower Memorial."[24]

How many of the forty-four total applications came from those thirty architects is unclear, as is whether any unsolicited firms made it past the first cut. The automatic exclusion of individuals and the tiny number of submissions ensured that someone like Maya Lin, at the time of her selection for the Vietnam Veterans Memorial a highly talented but not-yet-established designer, could never be considered for the memorial.

The forty-four applicants were whittled down to seven semi-finalists before the candidates were asked to provide "a brief sketch format submission,"[25] and it was only after the seven had been cut to a final four that firms were required to produce a "detailed design vision." Just down the Mall from the Martin Luther King Jr. Memorial, the design of which was selected from nine hundred proposals, the Eisenhower Memorial Commission had ensured that a memorial to Dwight Eisenhower would be built from one of just four design proposals. Previous commissions for memorials had understood that the process used by the Eisenhower Memorial Commission places the cart before the horse, because the design is of greatest importance in the creation of a memorial, not the firm that will produce it.

Each of the remaining firms was given a $50,000 stipend to develop a detailed design concept, and once they had produced these, a blind jury made up of three architects, two landscape architects, one urban designer, one information designer, one lighting designer, and an Eisenhower family representative considered the four concepts.[26] The blind jury ultimately decided that "None of the visions expressed the whole essence of Eisenhower. The schemes as presented were mediocre for such an important memorial. This memorial will be in DC for a very long time and its [sic] about a great man, it may be well worth the time and expense to have the two best teams do another round of design before deciding between them."[27] Despite this clear lack of enthusiasm for any of the submitted design proposals, and against the jury's recommendation to go through another round of designs, the GSA evaluation board (on which both David Eisenhower and Rocco Siciliano served) selected Gehry Partners, LLP, as the first-choice firm, while Krueck & Sexton Architects landed in the runner-up position.

This decision immediately raised concerns of favoritism and collusion, especially since the vote was not unanimous. In his written testimony to Congress in 2012, David Eisenhower wrote, "During the selection process for an architect, a number of 'jurors' including myself supported another architectural firm and did not vote to select Mr. Gehry as the architect."[28] Susan Eisenhower's statement at that hearing affirmed this, when she, writing on behalf of the Eisenhower family, noted, "Furthermore, David Eisenhower, while on the architectural jury selection, promoted another architectural firm other than Gehry Partners. It was a narrow vote, and the family's choice was defeated."[29] Though the actual votes are hidden from the American people, it is almost certain that David Eisenhower's vote differed from Rocco Siciliano's.

Critics noted not only Siciliano's frequent mentions of Gehry in Commission meetings and prior working relationship with him, but also that the competition had been explicitly designed to give Gehry's firm a good chance of winning. For example, the weights assigned to normal Design Excellence criteria for the selection of a designer were inexplicably changed for the Eisenhower Memorial competition. While Past Design Performance is typically weighted at 35 percent, Philosophy and Design Intent at 25 percent, the Lead Designer's Portfolio at 25 percent, and the Lead Designer's Résumé at 15 percent, for the Eisenhower Memorial the percentages were changed significantly. In the Eisenhower Memorial selection process, Past Design Performance counted for just 15 percent, Philosophy and Design Intent was reduced to 20 percent, Lead Designer Portfolio shot up all the way to 55 percent, and Lead Designer Profile (the replacement for Lead Designer's Résumé) was weighed at 10 percent.[30] The changes to the criteria could have only helped Gehry, as the many overbudget and problem-riddled buildings he has designed were made to count less than the star-studded nature of his portfolio.

Charges that the changes to the normal Design Excellence criteria were made to assist Gehry in obtaining the commission were rejected by Siciliano, but they were, and are, continually reiterated by the Eisenhower Memorial Commission's critics, foremost among them the National Civic Art Society. Dedicated to excellence and fitness of design in public buildings, the Society galvanized around the decision to hire Gehry and raised the issue of the memorial to a national level, generating hundreds of critical articles in national news media of all types.

The National Civic Art Society and other critics objected to what they saw as a rigged competition and also to the winner of that competition. In March 2009, when he was officially named the first-choice architect, Gehry was the world's most famous starchitect, celebrated for his disruptive, anti-traditional buildings. Critics were quick to point out that his style would be, to say the least, a jarring addition to the National Mall, a space famed for its classically inspired memorials and monuments. Moreover, federal architects from the late 1700s to the twentieth century tended to take inspiration from the buildings of the Greeks and Romans because they saw them as examples of earlier republics and were eager to use their styles and elements in their own structures.

Gehry, however, was not interested in harmonizing with this past and, in fact, sought a rupture with it. At a conference in 1994, he was quoted as saying, "Most of us believe in democracy, but the system has created a world that looks strange, chaotic, and different, and we do not like it. We are struggling and it is easier to go back to models which are more coherent and seem more seductive now...If we are to survive, we need to live in the present and try to work towards the future. I will reiterate what I have said many times: I cannot face my children if I tell them I have no more ideas and I have to copy something that happened before. It is like giving up and telling them there is no future for them."[31] Exactly what he means by "models" is unclear, but his statement that "we need to live in the present" and his inability to face his children if he has "to copy something that happened before," encapsulate his attitude toward the past, particularly the architectural past.

There were no architects who served as voting members on the Eisenhower Memorial Commission, although in 2005, at the same meeting when a site on Maryland Avenue was officially selected as the location for the memorial, it announced the hiring of an in-house architect, Daniel Feil.[32] In addition to the lack of a voting architect, no one on the Commission had demonstrated previous knowledge of the history of architecture or memorialization. Though several commissioners, most notably Sen. Daniel Inouye, had served on previous monument commissions, their comments recorded in the Eisenhower Memorial Commission meeting minutes suggest that these experiences gave them more an appreciation for bureaucratic pitfalls and hurdles than matters of history or art. Even when the Commission *did* retain the services of a historian (the head of the Legacy Committee, Louis Galambos, has received almost $140,000 for his role as a "Senior Advisor" to the committee), it appears that the history of the National Mall was never discussed in any depth. Galambos organized a report on Eisenhower's life and legacy, not a report on the history of memorialization, the McMillan Plan (a century-old plan for the development of the National Mall), or the history of the Mall.

Even without an extensive knowledge of the Mall's architectural history, when the eight politicians and four presidential appointees on the Eisenhower Memorial Commission glanced at the portfolio submitted by Gehry Partners, they would have realized that the structures included in it were the polar opposites of the elegant buildings and monuments of the National Mall. In fact, the design concept conceived by Gehry Partners was out of sync with just about everything of significance in Washington, D.C., from the office buildings where the Commission's political representatives worked to the Capitol where they voted. Upon seeing Gehry's proposal for the Eisenhower Memorial, some of the commissioners must have remembered an earlier, ill-fated attempt to erect one of Gehry's signature buildings in Washington.

The Corcoran Gallery of Art was a fine arts museum, the oldest in Washington, D.C., and it housed a superb collection of American painting and sculpture. The museum was, however, beset by long-standing financial problems, and, despite frequent fundraising galas and huge donations, the museum was forced to charge visitors an admission fee in a city where most museums are free, including the nearby Smithsonian museums. This, in turn, had an impact on the total number of visitors.

In 1999 the Corcoran's then-director, David Levy, announced the addition of a new wing to the original gallery, an elegant Beaux Arts building designed by Ernest Flagg. This new wing was to be designed by Frank Gehry, undoubtedly because Levy hoped that the fashionable architect would call attention to the Corcoran and attract more visitors.

The Corcoran is on Seventeenth Street NW, close to the White House, a hallowed example of federal neoclassicism, and the Eisenhower Executive Office Building, a magnificent Beaux Arts building of the late-nineteenth century. Gehry's design for the wing was a flamboyant titanium addition that clashed with the finely proportioned classical elements of the Corcoran building and its neighboring historic edifices. Despite sticking out like a sore thumb, his design was, amazingly, approved by the Commission of Fine Arts, the federal entity charged with ensuring good and proper design in the District of Columbia, including on the National Mall. This organization was also to play a role in the Eisenhower Memorial design process.

The $110 million initial cost for the addition soon rose to $170 million, not an unusual occurrence for Gehry's buildings. The rise in projected cost made little difference, however, because the Corcoran was unable to raise the money for this ambitious scheme.[33] When it became clear that the Gehry wing would not be constructed, Levy quit. The chairman of the Corcoran's board, after thanking Levy for his "passion" and "dedication" during his tenure, said that "his overwhelming commitment to the Gehry wing would have made it difficult for the museum, under his leadership, to make the adjustments it must make."[34]

Gehry reacted dismissively to the news that his mold-breaking wing was no longer going to be built, saying businessmen on museum boards are "used to keeping companies in the black, and when they see red ink, they don't understand that's the way every museum in the world is." With the museum not willing to go into massive debt to fund his design, he asked in an interview, "How are they going to find another director of any significant kind?"[35] Significant directors, by Gehry's logic, would be attracted only to institutions capable of handing over blank checks to designers like himself. The financial problems that had plagued the Corcoran for decades were only exacerbated by the Gehry debacle (especially after the Corcoran placed $17 million in his company's coffers for unused designs), and after limping along for a few more years, the museum was forced to close for good in 2014.[36]

The minutes of the Eisenhower Commission meetings show no mention of the Corcoran fiasco, but had any of the commissioners taken time to study it, they would have found that Gehry was no respecter of place or tradition, that cost overruns were part of the price paid for hiring him, that there was not sufficient appetite for his new wing among the Gallery's donors (some of whom certainly possessed the money to fund the wing), and that he was possessed of ample amounts of self-esteem. None of this information was hidden, and yet none of it dampened the Eisenhower Commission's eagerness to hire him.

The Eisenhower Memorial's opponents claim this to be the result of Siciliano's gerrymandering for Gehry, especially in his role on the Design Excellence evaluation board, but there was another factor at work: the commissioners' desire to be *au courant*. Like the director of the Corcoran Gallery, the commissioners were certainly swayed by the prospect of employing the then-most-famous architect in the world. Commissioner Alfred Geduldig, for example, celebrated Gehry's appointment at the March 31, 2009, meeting by saying that "Frank Gehry is the world's most accomplished architect, the 'Frank Lloyd Wright of the modern era.'"[37] The commissioners were convinced, one must surmise, that hiring the celebrated starchitect would prove that they were not troglodytes clinging to the antiquated past of previous, outdated memorials, and that they, like Gehry's other patrons from Bilbao to Los Angeles, were culturally savvy.

The concern that what Gehry produced might not be warmly greeted by the senators' and representatives' constituents, or by other Americans visiting Washington, does not appear to have been voiced in any meetings. From the inception of the memorial onward, there was minimal effort to seek wide public comment from the citizens whose tax dollars would pay for the memorial, perhaps because the commissioners guessed that, by and large, the comments would not be favorable.

From the start, Gehry's ideas for the Eisenhower Memorial revealed just how disruptive he planned to be. In the video that Gehry Partners submitted to the Design Excellence board before Gehry was officially chosen as the designer, Gehry introduced a plan to "make a translucent screen—like a tapestry—made out of metal *so that it required no maintenance.*"[38] This "metal tapestry" had nothing in common with the time-tested, dignified designs that surround the National Mall, yet it was this design concept that the evaluation board chose as their winner.

On March 25, 2010, the Eisenhower Memorial Commission met to review three design schemes created by Gehry and to pick a preferred design scheme from the three. With Gehry present, Siciliano offered a brief description of the schemes. "Chairman Siciliano," the minutes read,

> noted that one of these design schemes keeps open the segment of Maryland Avenue that bisects the memorial site. The Chairman noted that this scheme has been developed at the request of GSA, since approval for the street closure remains pending. Mr. Siciliano also noted that the scheme preferred by both the architect and the EMC staff was scheme number three, represented by the largest architectural models on display in the meeting room. Mr. Siciliano

observed that the preference of the architect and EMC staff bears
no relation to the cost of this particular scheme, though it is the
most expensive.[39]

Siciliano's choice to inform the commissioners of the architect's preference before voting seems like an intentional move
to influence the result. In addition, the minutes record that the
model for the design that Gehry preferred was larger than the
models for the other two designs (including the design "developed at the request of GSA"); perhaps he also put more effort and
detail into the larger model. Finally, as Siciliano noted, the scheme
that Gehry and the EMC staff preferred was the most expensive,
though without estimates for the other two schemes, it's impossible to say whether there was a substantial difference.

From the meeting minutes, we are able to ascertain that the
two design schemes not selected did not contain tapestries, but the
third scheme, the one selected by the Commission, did. Given that
the tapestries were the calling card of the initial design concept
that was selected by the GSA evaluation board, it seems strange
that Gehry would have submitted only one design scheme with
tapestries to the Commission; perhaps this was another way to
steer voting.

Speaking to the group, Gehry "informed the Commission of
his early conclusion that relief images in stone would be appropriate as a design element and he commented on the relative merits
of bronze versus stone as sculptural materials. He stated that the
sculpted reliefs would be twice human scale...He explained his
preference for the inclusion of large, backdrop tapestries depicting
scenes from Eisenhower's life, observing that tapestries have been
used to tell stories through the ages. He shared information in
regard to his inquiries to determine the most durable material for
the tapestries as well as his preliminary conclusion that stainless
steel wire would lend itself to this use."[40]

The metal "tapestries" Gehry proposed were to be enormous,

with the largest of the three to run parallel to the Department of Education building for almost the entirety of the site's southern border, a length of more than 400 feet. The tapestries, he told the commissioners, "will be hung within a colonnade of free-standing limestone columns." Though Gehry called these supports "columns,"[41] they more closely resembled the massive pillars supporting highway overpasses. Likewise, Gehry insisted that tapestries were an integral part of the history of memorials, but this, as an objective survey of memorials reveals, is untrue.

In any case, Gehry's firm received $650,000 from the Commission for something called "tapestry development."[42] One of the main selling points for the tapestry concept was its supposed convenience; according to the video that Gehry Partners submitted to GSA, the tapestries were to be designed so that they required no maintenance. As it would turn out, however, even several hundred thousand dollars couldn't settle the question of whether the tapestries would hold up for any substantial amount of time.

By invoking antecedents for his woven screens (tapestries) and pillars (columns), Gehry concocted a fictitious historical gloss for parts of his design that had no connection with past memorials or monuments. Perhaps he thought this would make his design seem somehow indebted to the National Mall's classical buildings and thus make it easier for potential critics to accept.

At any rate, the third design scheme was celebrated by the Commission and unanimously approved. This point is crucial, because at the time of its approval, David Eisenhower was still a member of the Commission and his sister Anne Eisenhower was also in attendance at that very meeting. David voted for and praised the design (he is recorded as saying "that he likes the free-standing columns in Gehry's design, as they seem to symbolize the upward emergence of the United States to world power in the mid-twentieth century"), and Anne is recorded as deeming the design "wonderful." In light of David's later opposition to the design, his support expressed here may seem confusing, but in his testimony to Congress in 2012, he explained his comments by writing, "Once the Gehry firm was chosen...I supported efforts to assure that a memorial be built. During my tenure, the commissioners were always assured that the designs were evolving, and that there was plenty of time for consultation."[43]

In fact, the design *was* evolving, though not necessarily in such a way as to further endear it to the Eisenhower family. In the next version of the preferred design scheme, the smaller screens and pillars were reoriented so that they now stood at right angles to the larger screen. The sculptural elements of the monuments (a small statue of Eisenhower as a boy and reliefs depicting his most important deeds) were to be enclosed by the screen, creating an "urban room." When unveiled, it was praised by several critics for its daring rethinking of a memorial on the National Mall. Philip Kennicott, the art and architecture critic for the *Washington Post*, provided some of the most damning praise possible when he applauded Gehry for "re-gendering" the vocabulary of memorialization.[44] Soon, however, strong opposition to the Commission's work was voiced, including by the Eisenhower family. This opposition centered on questions about the memorial's size, cost, and its design.

Gehry's design for the Eisenhower Memorial filled a great deal of the four-acre location on Maryland Avenue. The Washington Monument, the Jefferson Memorial, and the Lincoln Memorial would have fit within its boundaries with room to spare.[45] Opponents of the design saw a disconnect between the gigantism of the screens and pillars and the modest character of Dwight Eisenhower. They cited his distaste for nontraditional art and reasoned that he would be embarrassed by such a grandiose memorial by a transgressive architect like Gehry, especially since the memorial was purposefully designed to be at odds with the other memorials and monuments on the National Mall.

Susan Eisenhower, for example, testified in 2012 that her grandfather

> would have expected something far less dramatic, far less—he would have wanted something on a smaller scale, I believe. This is an enormous thing... These metal mesh curtains are actually 80 feet high. This is the size of an eight-story office building. And everyone visiting the Memorial will be dwarfed by these edifices. I do not think he would understand it, and I do not think that it would appeal to him because he was well-known not to have much time for modern art. And as a matter of fact, my sister Anne and I could tell you a funny story about riding along in the Gettysburg countryside with him, both on different occasions, with Granddad saying that he hated billboards.[46]

Gehry's billboard-like tribute to Ike, then, is almost certainly the last thing the president would have wanted. Of course, it was exactly this ostentatious flaunting of tradition and history, as well as his penchant for grandiose scale, that had made Gehry the darling of elite patrons and critics in the first place.

Opponents of the design also claimed that the memorial's $150 million price tag was out of keeping with Eisenhower's reputation for fiscal restraint, especially in light of Gehry's cost overruns at other projects. There were, in addition, serious questions about the durability of the design; the metal screens, it was argued, would collect debris left by visitors to the National Mall and, more than likely, quickly deteriorate. These fears, too, were grounded in Gehry's past.

Gehry's firm was sued by the Massachusetts Institute of Technology (MIT) for negligence and breach of contract after the $300 million Ray and Maria Stata Center quickly developed problems ranging from cracked masonry to mold growth. After the case was settled in 2010, the counsel for the construction firm employed by MIT to build the Stata Center noted that the issues

FIGURE 1.2   THE STATA CENTER

Source: Wikimedia Commons

MIT's Stata Center, designed by Frank Gehry

at the heart of the case were "primarily of design as opposed to construction."[47] In response to the lawsuit, Gehry commented that the issues were "fairly minor," and claimed that "MIT is after our insurance."[48]

Aside from issues of cost and size, Gehry also attracted criticism for the depiction of Dwight Eisenhower that he chose to include in the memorial. Gehry's preference to include a statue of Ike as a "barefoot boy," rather than as the man who led armies and a country, riled many, including some of the Eisenhower family. David Eisenhower's letter to Congress in 2012 mentions how this feature played a role in turning him against the design, as he wrote, "I did not know the details of how the 'barefoot boy' theme was developing and I recognized the need to be in full consultation with the rest of my family...I am in full support of the family's decision to share our concerns with the public, and I endorse the family's efforts to gain a thorough review of the currently proposed design, including a redesign."[49]

The most important, and most voiced, protest, however, had

less to do with any one feature of Gehry's design than with the very nature of what a memorial should *be*. The world's great memorials are able to convey a sense of the character and deeds of the men and women they honor and inspire those who view them to do great things themselves. A good example of this is the Lincoln Memorial. Placed before a reflecting pool, with a view of the Capitol in the distance, it is reached by climbing a long flight of steps. This lengthy ascent creates a sense of unfolding drama as visitors rise toward the shrine-like building fronted with classically inspired columns through which they at last glimpse the large statue of a brooding Abraham Lincoln. All the elements—stairs, columns, and statue—brilliantly create a feeling of awe and reverence for the martyred president. The Vietnam Veterans Memorial is also moving and effective, but in a very different way. A black granite wall set into a deep trench, it is inscribed with the names of those who fell in the war. Visitors not only read these names, but also see their own reflections in the glossy stone. Inspired by Sir Edwin Lutyens's stark Cenotaph, a memorial to the dead of World War I in London, Maya Lin's design encourages meditation and reflection on loss rather than the martial aspects of the conflict.

With time, these great memorials have become landmarks, and both are now sacred civic spaces on the National Mall. From the civil rights rallies at the Lincoln Memorial (the venue of the famous "I Have a Dream" speech) to the annual pilgrimage of veterans and their families to the Vietnam Memorial, they are etched in America's memory and, not surprisingly, are the most visited memorials in Washington. Gehry's Eisenhower Memorial, its critics lament, is the opposite of these great memorials. Its piers, screens, plinths, and various other elements do not add up to a unified whole. They convey no lasting emotion; they lack drama, even coherence.

By the time that Gehry's designs began to circulate around Washington, whispers about the amount of money that the

Eisenhower Memorial Commission had already blown through were turning into louder grumbles. Even before reviewing Gehry's design, the Commission had spent many millions of taxpayer dollars; the original $300,000 appropriation was simply the first and smallest in a long series.

For almost the first decade of its existence, the Commission did not possess the authority to directly hire staff, so the Eisenhower Memorial Commission was staffed by GSA-coordinated "consultants" under the command of EMC Executive Director Carl Reddel. Reddel (a former chief executive of the Eisenhower Institute) has received a salary in excess of $150,000 a year since at least 2009; his salary from 2001 to 2008 is unavailable.[50] Reddel's staff, housed in an expensive K Street office suite, has fluctuated between eight and eleven full-time workers. We have complete salary data for only two years: 2016, when the staff was paid $706,541, and 2015, when the staff was paid $835,706.[51]

For almost the first decade of the Commission's life, the staff salaries and expenses were funded by relatively small, semiregular appropriations ($1.75 million in 2001, $2.6 million in 2002, etc.).[52] Once Gehry was selected, however, and the prospect of building became more concrete, the appropriations ramped up: the Eisenhower Memorial Commission received $19 million for FY 2010 and $32.99 million for FY 2012. By 2013, however, amid public backlash to Gehry's design, enthusiasm for large appropriations began to wane, and the Commission received only $2.1 million for FY 2013.

This amount was further reduced for FY 2014 when the Commission was given only $1 million rather than the $51 million it requested.[53] The bad news continued to mount for the Eisenhower Memorial in April 2014, when the National Capital Planning Commission (NCPC) rejected Gehry's design, saying that it would not complement surrounding buildings and that the eighty-foot-tall limestone columns supporting the tapestries would compromise or eliminate views of the Capitol.[54]

By mid-2014, then, a total of $65,440,000 had been appropriated for the building of Gehry's Eisenhower Memorial (around $41 million of which had been spent or obligated), and the Eisenhower Memorial Commission still did not even possess an approved design.[55] Gehry Partners had received more than $16 million for design support and other work related to design. (Gehry has always claimed that he worked pro bono, but the funds for design, concept development, and construction documents were paid to his firm.)[56] Paying for final construction drawings (which alone cost more than $1.7 million) before the many approvals needed to build on the National Mall were granted was a questionable procedure because it ensured that the architect would be paid even if his work never saw the light of day, as happened with the Corcoran Gallery wing. Furthermore, because there were certainly going to be changes (and there were) to the design as it went through the approval process, the so-called final drawings would need substantial modifications (and they did), which would further inflate the cost and the amount of money paid to Gehry's firm.

The glacial pace of the Commission and the amount of money it had already spent was exposed in a scathing report created by the House Committee on Natural Resources under the direction of Rep. Doc Hastings (then-chairman) and Rep. Rob Bishop. Released on July 25, 2014, amid mounting problems for the Commission, *A Five-Star Folly: An Investigation into the Cost Increases, Construction Delays, and Design Problems That Have Been a Disservice to the Effort to Memorialize Dwight D. Eisenhower* issued criticism all around, from the commissioners to the designer to GSA.

The report expressed skepticism about the way the Commission chose Gehry, noting that the process used to select Gehry Partners "substantially deviated from the standard Design Excellence Program, and the factors used to select the designer were weighted in a way that benefited a well-known designer such as Gehry."[57] It also laid blame at the feet of Gehry, specifically for his refusal to meet well-established design mandates. "The criteria necessary for any Memorial design," the report states, "were clearly laid out as early as 2006, yet the design Gehry continues to propose and the Commission supports fails to meet those required design principles…The design continues to fall short of…the requirements of the Commemorative Works Act. Given these ongoing shortcomings, the design has not yet received the approvals necessary to begin construction."[58]

A Five-Star Folly also zeroed in on the Commission's handling of its appropriated funds and its failure to raise private money. From the earliest meetings, it was clear that Rocco Siciliano wanted the memorial to be federally funded. At the Commission's fourth meeting, on February 28, 2002, the meeting minutes record that Siciliano "expressed the view that he would like to see federal funding for the memorial itself and was optimistic about the timetable of five to seven years if the memorial is federally funded."[59] As time went on, and the appropriations environment changed, however, the idea of the construction of the memorial being funded by "a public-private mix," in the words of Eisenhower Memorial Committee Executive Architect Daniel Feil, began to appear more attractive to the commission.[60]

The Commission chose to order a fundraising feasibility study from The Webster Group in March 2008. As is noted in *A Five-Star Folly*, "The Webster Group submitted its Preliminary Fundraising Feasibility Study Report to the Eisenhower Commission on April 11, 2008, recommending for further study a preliminary fundraising goal of $45 million, of which $36 million would cover 45 percent of an assumed $80 million in construction costs and $9 million in fundraising expenses. Under this scenario, Congress would have been expected to appropriate $44 million to cover the remaining construction costs. The preliminary report also recommended the Commission establish a separate non-profit group with tax-exempt status to receive donations."[61]

The Commission was intrigued enough to order a more detailed feasibility study. This study was delivered in 2010, after

Gehry had been chosen as the lead designer for the Eisenhower Memorial, and while America was in the grips of the Great Recession. This report was less optimistic about the Commission's ability to raise tens of millions of dollars from private sources, saying, "The current economic downturn was a key factor in the attitudes of potential donors for this study, particularly in regard to the proposed $50 million goal, which seems excessive to many...Given the constraints now faced by the Eisenhower Memorial Commission, including leadership and economic climate, $10 to $15 million is recommended as an achievable goal."[62] Gehry's star power was, apparently, less able to galvanize support and funding than the Commission had initially believed. As the detailed feasibility study noted, "Individuals interviewed feel the price tag was much too high for the memorial, and there is concern that the architect chosen will result in even higher costs. Generally, in projects like this, the cost escalates because people start to embellish the design and/or plan, which further exacerbates the budget and time frame."[63] How prophetic those concerns turned out to be!

It was only a week after The Webster Group issued their detailed feasibility study, and, in it, made clear the limited prospects for private fundraising, that the Commission met to review Gehry's three design concepts and, as we know, chose the most expensive scheme. At that meeting, in Gehry's presence, Siciliano "stated that he hopes for maximum federal support, that precedent exists for 100 percent federal funding of presidential memorials in the case of the Lincoln, Jefferson, and Theodore Roosevelt Memorials, and that federal funding had encompassed 89 percent of the cost of the Franklin D. Roosevelt Memorial and 65 percent of the cost of the John F. Kennedy Center for the Performing Arts. The chairman stated that the design phase of the Eisenhower Memorial's development will last two years, and that the fundraising efforts must begin soon, since the Commission must have all the funding in hand before construction can begin. Chairman

FIGURE 1.3a   AERIAL VIEW

Aerial view of the proposed Dwight D. Eisenhower Memorial

FIGURE 1.3b   TAPESTRY VIEW

Tapestry views of the proposed Dwight D. Eisenhower Memorial

Siciliano stated that it had been the Commission's historic intention to seek 100 percent federal funding, though planning for
private-sector fundraising is already under way."[64]

Nowhere in Siciliano's comments to the Commission is there
mention of The Webster Group's damning find that a goal of only
$10 to $15 million in private funding was feasible for the project;
either Siciliano hadn't read the report, or perhaps, having seen the
report, simply decided it was easier to push for full federal funding
(regardless of the appropriations environment or financial burden

FIGURE 1.4 EMC APPROPRIATIONS HISTORY

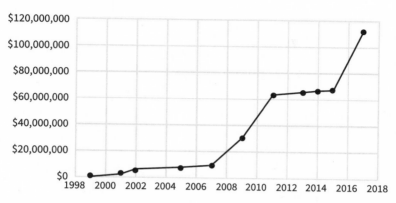

This graph depicts the accumulated total of federal appropriations by year.

it would place on the American taxpayer) to get his memorial built than to undergo the hassle of extensive fundraising efforts. It is also important to note his admission that "the Commission must have all the funding in hand before construction can begin." This requirement is a provision of the Commemorative Works Act, though, on occasion, projects are granted waivers to allow them to begin construction without all funds in hand. Such a waiver was eventually granted to the Eisenhower Memorial Commission, but, amid rising opposition to the project, it was actually rescinded in 2014.[65]

The Commission did, eventually, take a stab at fundraising. On March 4, 2011, GSA chose to award a fundraising contract to Odell, Simms & Lynch, Inc. (OSL). According to *A Five-Star Folly*, the base contract was for only $182,500, but it came with options worth $3,150,000. After developing a fundraising plan, the first contract option allowed OSL to "launch the fundraising campaign with a goal of raising $7 million over 10 months. The value of this task was originally listed as $615,000. Under the second option (referred to as Task 3 in the contract), valued at $375,000, OSL was to raise another $4 million over the following six months. Under the remaining options (referred to as Tasks 4 to 7), which would kick in over the next 35 months and be worth almost $2.2 million, OSL was to raise $24 million—for a total of $35 million by spring 2015."[66]

In a project where almost every contract that the Commission had entered into was modified several times to cost taxpayers millions in additional dollars, it is no surprise that OSL's contract and goals were constantly modified as the Commission paid more and more for less and less. By the middle of 2014, OSL was nowhere near reaching even the first major funding milestone, $7 million. In fact, when *A Five-Star Folly* was issued, OSL had managed to raise only $448,164, even though it had received more than $1.2 million for fundraising work. Amazingly, after more than three years of fundraising work, OSL had managed to be paid more than two and a half times the amount of money they'd raised for the Eisenhower Memorial.[67]

The Commission, of course, had responses for why the fundraising efforts went so poorly. They attempted to lay the blame at the feet of those in Congress and members of the public who continued to oppose the proposed memorial. The attempt to deflect the mounting criticism was unsuccessful, and by the time *A Five-Star Folly* was released in late July 2014, the Commission's construction authority had been revoked through FY 2014. Even in 2015, when the National Capital Planning Commission voted to approve Gehry's revised design, both the House and the Senate seemed united against the project. Rep. Rob Bishop, one of the figures behind *A Five-Star Folly*, put the matter plainly when he said, "Whether or not the current design is approved by the commission has little relevance to the prospects of congressional funding."[68] With the Eisenhower family united against the design, and critics continuing to question the choices of the Eisenhower Memorial Commission, the approval of the design by a board of unelected bureaucrats (the Planning Commission) simply wasn't enough to get Congress to reopen the checkbook.

As the issue of funding loomed over the Eisenhower Memorial

Commission, another momentous change took place. In 2015 Rocco Siciliano stepped down from the chairmanship of the Eisenhower Commission (he remained a voting member) and Sen. Pat Roberts of Kansas, a longtime supporter, was elected chairman in a Commission meeting that lacked a quorum.[69] Upon being named chairman, Roberts compared the effort to build the memorial to a battle, quoting Eisenhower by saying that in the struggle to build, "We will accept nothing less than full victory."[70]

Soon after taking over as chairman, Roberts enlisted the help of Bob Dole, a former senator and presidential candidate. Dole, who had been the national chairman of the World War II Memorial Campaign, enlarged the Commission's advisory board to include notable public servants and entertainment figures, including former vice president Al Gore, former secretary of state Donald Rumsfeld, and actor Tom Hanks (with whom Dole had previously worked to fundraise for the National World War II Memorial). Dole advocated for a speedy completion of the Gehry design; urgency, he claimed, was in order because the memorial needed to be completed in time for remaining World War II veterans to visit it. While this is an admirable wish, it ignores the fact that those who served in that conflict already had a huge monument on the National Mall and that many servicemen did not serve under Eisenhower, instead serving under other officers in other theaters of war.

Although the commissioners, taken as a whole, did not have a track record of taking criticism of their efforts well (Siciliano, amid criticism of the design from the Eisenhower family, including Dwight Eisenhower's son John, is reported to have written, "I am one person who feels competent to say that he believes President Eisenhower would be most pleased as to what the present Commissioners have unanimously accepted"[71]), Dole brought a new level of absurdity to his defense of the memorial. In one letter published in *Roll Call*, he disjointedly argued that the only persons who could criticize the memorial were combat veterans, because others "don't know what it's like to be at the receiving end of a howitzer, or know what it is to fight a real war," ignoring the real procedural and aesthetic problems that plagued the project.[72] Dole's clumsy equation of war with monument building was intended to quell dissent, but it became just one more piece of ammunition that critics could use against the Commission.

More importantly, Dole seemed to ignore the fact that memorials and monuments are not only for the living, but for rising generations as well, generations that will have little or no knowledge of the past. To be effective and memorable, they need to communicate the importance of who they memorialize. Dole's, and the commissioners', presentist view of the Eisenhower Memorial ignores this crucial element.

With fundraising stalled, appropriations cut to a trickle, the waiver to the Federal Commemorative Works Act rescinded, and a staunch legion of critics dug in, the Eisenhower Memorial project seemed destined for the waste-bin of history. Then, in September 2016, the unthinkable happened: the Eisenhower family (most importantly, *Susan* Eisenhower) flipped. Former secretary of state James A. Baker III, a member of the Eisenhower Memorial Commission Advisory Committee, had been dispatched to negotiate with the family, and, by hook or by crook, he successfully brought the Eisenhower family back into the fold.

In an article on the flip, Susan is quoted as writing to Baker, "While some of us may have had other preferences in the past, all of us support your proposal... We are also pleased that the idea of the young Kansas boy is appropriately featured on the memorial site."[73] Another article adds, "We recognize that your recommendation offers a compromise, one which all Americans who loved the general and the president can support."[74]

For a supposed compromise, it appears that Gehry gave little ground. Gehry's "tapestries" concept, likened by Susan Eisenhower in her congressional testimony to an "Iron Curtain" and "concentration camp chain-link fences," now appeared to have her blessing.[75] The only design features of substance that had changed since her first voicing her disapproval of the design were the number of tapestries in the proposed design (after NCPC did not approve any of the three Gehry designs in 2011, Gehry had dropped the minor east and west tapestries[76]) and the imagery on the remaining tapestry. (Gehry decided to change the image "from a composite view of Abilene, Kansas to a contemporary peacetime image of the beach at Normandy, France.")[77]

Susan Eisenhower's reversal is nearly inexplicable in light of almost a decade of tension between her and the Commission, especially Siciliano. Eisenhower had, after all, given up her role at the Eisenhower Institute so that the living memorial study could proceed without accusation of personal gain; from the meeting minutes after the report was delivered, we can see that Eisenhower basically gave up her job for nothing. Any reasonable person is forced to conclude that Baker must have held powerful bargaining chips when he met with the Eisenhower family. Perhaps he emphasized that the memorial was at a now-or-never stage, and if the family continued to fight, their grandfather would never receive a monument on the Mall. The Swamp is, by nature, murky, and the stories that come from it are almost never complete.

Returning to the visible outcomes of the Baker–Eisenhower solution (perhaps *pact* is a better word), the changes made to appease the Eisenhower family were head scratchers: on the scrim, the trees and leaves were replaced with a photograph-like panoramic view of a Normandy beach, the site of one of the D-Day landings by forces commanded by the Supreme Allied Commander, Gen. Dwight Eisenhower. But, inexplicably, the beach is empty and peaceful, without any reference to the heroic struggle of Eisenhower's troops or, indeed, anything related to World War II. What the viewer would see is a stretch of beach that could be anywhere. Tests and surveys prove that Americans know little about even the most important documents and figures of their history, so it's reasonable to assume that they would have no idea about the connection between an anodyne beach and the wartime accomplishment of Dwight Eisenhower.

Because the memorial is not self-explanatory, it will need descriptive texts for visitors to understand what it depicts. This is an obvious failure, because a great memorial explains itself. The Lincoln and Jefferson memorials, for example, convey a sense of drama and importance that needs no help from written texts. The Eisenhower Memorial Commission has paid $2 million for an "e-memorial" (a combination of digital media and a smartphone application) that visitors will need to consult, at home or at the memorial itself, to understand something about the man it honors.

At some point between the Baker–Eisenhower agreement and September 2017, the design on the tapestry changed yet again. Although the language in the releases about the Eisenhower family's approval suggested that the view of the Normandy beach would be realistic, the final design submission given to the NCPC on September 1, 2017, says, "After further study and review of the previous tapestry mockups, the team concluded that a graphic approach to the Normandy landscape art with higher contrast would be more successful for improving image clarity against the backdrop of the Lyndon B. Johnson building. The revised design is an artistic drawing of the cliffs of Normandy coastline that will increase legibility and the transparency of the overall tapestry."[78]

The released "design" is a series of giant squiggly lines much like the famous doodles that Gehry draws for the earliest conceptions of his buildings. Perhaps these are his abstract translation of the realistic Normandy scene, or maybe they are just his gigantic signature sprawled across 440 feet of woven stainless-steel screen.

The site's final design was still not settled after the Eisenhower family went back on board. For example, a statue of Ike as a young man was moved, then moved again, after the Commission of Fine Arts rejected an attempt to move it to a promenade behind the "tapestry."[79] Concerns about the Capitol viewshed led to reductions in the numbers of columns and trees in the design. By the fall of 2017, however, the end of the bureaucratic process seemed to have been reached. With a fresh $45 million of appropriated funds, the Eisenhower Memorial Commission was almost ready to break ground.

In September 2017, the final design, which was met with instant ridicule and head-shaking incredulity by the public, was approved unanimously by the Commission of Fine Arts, whose members are appointed by the president of the United States for four-year terms.[80] At the end of the meeting, after the vote, chairman Earl Powell III, according to *Roll Call*, leaned across the table and told his colleagues, "Now we can say it hasn't been 17 wasted years."[81] It's troubling that after all of the struggles and controversies that surrounded every step of the Eisenhower Memorial process the chairman of the Commission of Fine Arts still appeared to regard success as producing *a* monument rather than producing *the right* memorial. It's strange that Powell, who has been a guardian of tradition and excellence since becoming director of the National Gallery of Art in 1992, was supportive of the radically disruptive Gehry design. It's also interesting to note that the Gallery's budget comes from the House of Representatives Subcommittee on the Interior, Environment, and Related Agencies, whose chairman, Rep. Ken Calvert, enthusiastically supported funding after the Baker–Eisenhower pact was finalized. Whether Powell's dependence on that subcommittee for Gallery funds could be seen as a conflict of interest is an open question; certainly if he had thought this to be the case, he would have had every right to recuse himself from any matter that involved his institution's congressional appropriations.

In October 2017, the NCPC gave its own approval to the updated design, and, with a waiver in hand allowing building to begin without possessing all necessary funds (the Commission managed to receive another waiver after being stripped in 2014), the Eisenhower Memorial Commission saw ground broken for the project on November 2, 2017.[82]

In the end, it looks as if the American people will receive a monument by committee, one that has involved the input of no less than a dozen distinct commissions, agencies, and councils. More than fifteen years after the Eisenhower Memorial Commission first received taxpayer funds, the public conversation remains about that body's missteps rather than about the man for whom the memorial will ostensibly be made, and that might be the saddest part of it all: when all is said and done, the National Mall will have a monument to Frank Gehry rather than Dwight D. Eisenhower.

✤ CHAPTER 2 ✤

Art in Architecture

The unaccountable, complex, and opaque bureaucratic morass in Washington that brought the American people the Eisenhower Memorial is also responsible for spending millions more dollars on art across the country through the General Services Administration's little-known but decades-old Art in Architecture program. Although the Eisenhower Memorial selection process was an outrageous example of the work that can be done in the Swamp, it was really no more than General Services Administration (GSA) gets away with on a regular basis with its Art in Architecture scheme, which requires that at least .5 percent of the total construction cost for every new federal building and every substantial renovation project be spent on something broadly defined as "art."

Von Rydingsvard's *Cedrus*

A look at one such piece of art, installed in Miramar, Florida, in 2015, shows just how badly an Art in Architecture commission can turn out. Ursula von Rydingsvard's *Cedrus*, a seventeen-foot-tall, eight-ton sculpture made from imported western red cedar, passed all of the Art in Architecture program's panels, boards, and evaluations, and yet the $750,000 statue lasted less than a year in the lobby of the Benjamin P. Grogan and Jerry L. Dove Federal Building before it was removed.

The first Art in Architecture meeting for the building, a new headquarters for the FBI in south Florida, was held in August 2010. Although there are only seven official members of any Art in Architecture panel, fourteen people attended this meeting, including five GSA employees. The building's lead architects were Krueck & Sexton, the firm, you might recall, listed as the second-choice designer for the Eisenhower Memorial. For the new facility, Krueck & Sexton had designed an angled glass and steel structure that fit perfectly with GSA's Design Excellence program's portfolio. In Mark Sexton's opening statement to the panel, he noted that he favored "exterior artwork over interior artwork, as artwork installed outdoors could have a greater impact in terms of public accessibility."[1] Accessibility, one can surmise, is something that should be a key factor in the planning of art paid for by the taxpayers.

The FBI's two representatives at the meeting echoed Sexton's comments, one saying "that the FBI would like an artist who could focus on the landscape or [a] proposed water element," while the other added "that the FBI wants to have attractive artwork for their employees to enjoy, but they do not want the artwork to serve as a destination for the public."[2] The FBI, clearly, did not want the artwork to serve as a distraction or draw attention to the facility, which makes a great deal of sense. Any of GSA's usual postmodern, gimmicky artworks would have gone against their wishes.

After the meeting, the panel members nominated a combined total of thirty-eight artists for the commission, presumably focusing their attention on artists capable of acting on the architect's ideas for a work outside of the building. At the next meeting, held in November 2010, however, the architects seem to have changed their minds. The meeting notes record that "Before the panel began reviewing artist's [sic] slides, the architects clarified that the landscape design is part of the design concept and will be executed by the selected builder. Natural moving water will be a feature of the site; however, a water feature could be a maintenance concern, and a water event was deemed not appropriate."[3] With the architect's "clarification," then, the criteria for an "acceptable" artist shifted dramatically, yet the list of artists up for consideration remained the same. We don't know exactly what occurred during the deliberations at the second meeting (the notes were not given to us by GSA), but, by the end of the session, the panel had recommended three artists be considered for the commission: Ursula von Rydingsvard, Paula Hayes, and Teresita Fernández.

In the subsequent evaluation performed by the Technical Evaluation Board, von Rydingsvard was given a score of 9.86 out of 10, far ahead of the 8.57 given to the other two finalists.[4] We do not know how GSA arrived at such precise numbers, because, again, the notes were withheld, though other cases have shown that there is no rhyme or reason that governs the assignment of a score.[5] A coherent design proposal was not the driving factor in forming these scores, because the Art in Architecture program doesn't ask for any design proposal before choosing an artist. This cannot be considered anything but a huge flaw in the selection process.

The third panel meeting, where Von Rydingsvard presented her final concept, was held on February 4, 2014, with nineteen people in attendance.[6] She presented previous examples of her work (some of which appear almost identical to *Cedrus*[7]) and expressed her intention to locate the massive cedar sculpture in the main lobby. There was no significant debate at the meeting. No one questioned Von Rydingsvard's materials or design. Only a few questions were asked about the placement; real concern was expressed regarding only the potential for litter to be thrown into the sculpture. The FBI representative at the meeting is recorded as speaking only twice, neither time expressing support for the design proposal. While there is no record of an official vote, the regional commissioner's letter to the chief architect recommending fabrication, dated February 19, 2014, claims that the "panel unanimously approved the final concept."

The public story of *Cedrus* begins where the meeting records and authorization letters end. Soon after the piece arrived in Florida in early 2015, it began to attract attention for all of the wrong reasons. As a *Politico* article from December 2016 succinctly explains, "Shortly after *Cedrus* arrived, FBI workers began getting sick, including at least a dozen who were hospitalized...Most suffered allergic reactions to cedar dust coming off the sculpture. Among those who became sick was the office's only nurse, who had to be relocated to another office."[8]

The records for the Art in Architecture meetings include no mention of the allergenic properties of cedar dust, which is staggering considering that Von Rydingsvard is herself allergic to cedar and must wear a protective suit with an attached air pump just to work with the material. A 2013 National Public Radio interview with Von Rydingsvard notes, "After all these years, she's become allergic to the cedar. She has to wear a 15-pound suit with air pumped into it for as many as eight hours a day."[9] The known effects of western red cedar exposure aren't limited to a runny nose; one database of wood toxicity notes that the effects of exposure include "asthma, nervous system effects, [and] NPC [nasopharyngeal carcinoma, more commonly known as throat cancer] (rare)."[10] No wonder Von Rydingsvard takes such pains to protect herself.

Cedar dust was not the only allergen present in the new FBI facility. The Federal Occupational Health (FOH) agency conducted air-quality tests several months after complaints began to come out of the facility; though they did not find abnormally high levels of cedar dust in the building (which was to be expected, given that several attempts had been made to clean the statue and surrounding areas), they *did* detect elevated levels of formaldehyde, one of the main ingredients in a glue that Von Rydingsvard used to coat *Cedrus*. Formaldehyde, unlike plicatic acid (the chief allergen in western red cedar), is a volatile gas, so it is certain that the levels of formaldehyde in the facility were even higher before the tests were conducted.

The FBI, justifiably alarmed at the allergic reactions, requested that GSA, the owner of *Cedrus* and all other Art in Architecture commissions, remove the sculpture from the facility. Incredibly, GSA refused to comply with the request and even objected when the FBI had *Cedrus* wrapped in tarps to stop the spread of cedar dust. A months-long argument erupted, with GSA refusing to pay for the removal of *Cedrus* and denying responsibility for the sicknesses. In an angry letter sent to Public Buildings Service (one of GSA's three divisions) Commissioner Norman Dong after *Cedrus* was finally removed, FBI CFO Richard Haley wrote,

> The health and safety issues surrounding the sculpture were real… while we are relieved that the artwork has now been removed, we feel it is incumbent upon us to inform you that the customer service received from GSA Southeast Regional Commissioner Michael Goodwin in dealing with this matter was less than satisfactory. Mr. Goodwin resisted the FBI's requests to remove the artwork, inexplicably ignoring that 17 Miami field office employees became ill following its installation. Rather than expressing concern for the FBI's ever sickening workforce, Mr. Goodwin appeared to be concerned only for the artwork. He even went so far as to suggest that the FBI "endangered" the artwork by wrapping it in a tarp in an attempt to protect field office employees. To add insult to injury, Mr. Goodwin required the FBI to pay $411,358 for the removal of the sculpture—an artwork the FBI did not request, and, in fact, opposed due to the high cost to the taxpayer ($750,000 plus building modifications).[11]

As Haley mentioned, GSA's eventual concurrence that *Cedrus* needed to be removed was not based on compassionate grounds or a rational acknowledgment of the threat posed by the cedar sculpture, but on fears for the safety of the *artwork*. A memo

FIGURE 2.1   MEMO FROM J. GIBSON TO N. DONG

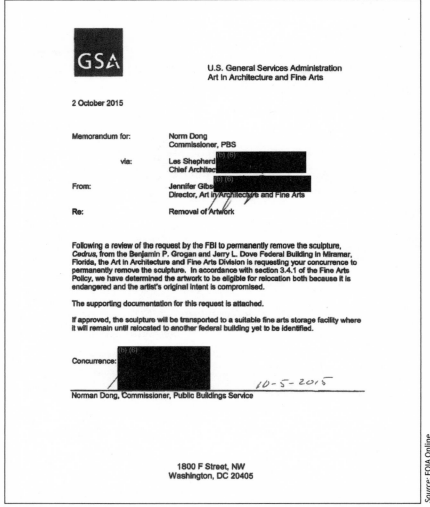

GSA

U.S. General Services Administration
Art in Architecture and Fine Arts

2 October 2015

Memorandum for: Norm Dong
                         Commissioner, PBS

                via: Les Shepherd
                         Chief Architect

From: Jennifer Gibson
                         Director, Art in Architecture and Fine Arts

Re: Removal of Artwork

Following a review of the request by the FBI to permanently remove the sculpture,
Cedrus, from the Benjamin P. Grogan and Jerry L. Dove Federal Building in Miramar,
Florida, the Art in Architecture and Fine Arts Division is requesting your concurrence to
permanently remove the sculpture. In accordance with section 3.4.1 of the Fine Arts
Policy, we have determined the artwork to be eligible for relocation both because it is
endangered and the artist's original intent is compromised.

The supporting documentation for this request is attached.

If approved, the sculpture will be transported to a suitable fine arts storage facility where
it will remain until relocated to another federal building yet to be identified.

Concurrence: _____ 10-5-2015
Norman Dong, Commissioner, Public Buildings Service

1800 F Street, NW
Washington, DC 20405

Memo from Jennifer Gibson to Norman Dong with the subject line "Removal of Artwork"

from Art in Architecture Director Jennifer Gibson to Norman
Dong recommending removal does not mention the sicknesses at
the FBI building, but simply claims that the statue is eligible for
removal "both because it is endangered and because the artist's
original intent has been compromised." Moreover, the memo
further states that if the removal is approved "the sculpture will

be transported to a suitable fine arts storage facility where it will remain until relocated to another federal building yet to be identified."[12]

To make this relocation possible, Michael Goodwin, the regional commissioner who provided "less than satisfactory" customer service to the FBI, explicitly suggested to another GSA employee that they solicit a "clean bill of health" for the piece from FOH, saying that it was important to avoid "political fallout from relocating a potential health risk from one place to another."[13] He made it clear that in the process of soliciting this clean bill of health "employees" should not be surveyed. The "employees" to whom he refers are certainly the tenants of the FBI building who might dispute the results based on personal experiences. The entire memo is shot through with a blatant disregard for the citizens who pay for the Art in Architecture program and are supposed to be served by it.

The emails, doctors' notes, letters, air-quality reports, and meeting minutes, all taken together, bring us back to a basic truth: *Cedrus* should never have been commissioned. The fact that it *was* commissioned indicates that the process by which Art in Architecture artwork is selected is fatally flawed. With Von Rydingsvard's sculpture, there was a clear lack of fit (an abstract sculpture made of Canadian wood by a New York–based artist hardly harmonizes with a new, glass-filled facility in south Florida) in addition to the obvious lack of critical thought about the materials and placement. It is easy to agree with Mr. Haley's assertion in his letter to Commissioner Dong that the battle over *Cedrus* "clearly demonstrate[s] misplaced priorities and [is] inconsistent with GSA's stated goal to be 'a model for outstanding customer service in the Government.'"[14]

Serra's *Tilted Arc*

The *Cedrus* fiasco was presaged by an earlier skirmish between the public and GSA over another controversial work: Richard Serra's

Tilted Arc, a 120-foot-long, 12-foot-tall wall of COR-TEN steel installed in Federal Plaza in front of the Jacob K. Javits Federal Building in Manhattan. When *Tilted Arc* was installed in 1981, there was, predictably, a chorus of complaints about the work, especially from the federal employees working inside the Javits Building. It intersected the plaza, blocked views, and impeded pedestrian traffic through the plaza. The open space once enjoyed by federal employees was now cleaved by a gigantic and intimidating wall of rusting steel.

Serra, in the same vein as Frank Gehry, is a willfully disruptive artist, and, like the designer of the Eisenhower Memorial, is a darling of the rarefied world of avant-garde art critics. *Tilted Arc* was as hostile to the enjoyment of Federal Plaza as the Eisenhower Memorial is to the National Mall, and purposely so; even before he received his commission, Serra spoke candidly on his disdain for "functional" works of art, saying, "There seems to be in this country, right now, especially in sculpture, a tendency to make work which attends to architecture. I am not interested in work which is structurally ambiguous, or in sculpture which satisfies urban design principles... I am interested in sculpture which is non-utilitarian, non-functional... any use is a misuse."[15]

The federal workers inside of the Javits Building, however, did not appreciate Serra's "non-utilitarian, non-functional" intrusion into their lives. Within a year, 1,300 of them had signed a petition demanding that GSA remove *Tilted Arc*. Debate continued to grow over the prospect of removal until a hearing was called in 1985. After hearing testimony from Serra and the various stakeholders both for and against removal, GSA officials voted four to one to remove *Tilted Arc*.

Tilted Arc could not, however, simply be shuttled to a new location for display; Serra argued that the piece was site-specific and would therefore lose its meaning if GSA moved it. He sued GSA to keep *Tilted Arc* in the plaza in front of the Jacob K. Javits

Federal Building and, in doing so, set off a series of legal battles and public debates that lasted for years.

By spring of 1989, however, Serra had exhausted all legal avenues for keeping *Tilted Arc* in Federal Plaza. On March 15, 1989, *Tilted Arc* was finally removed from Federal Plaza. The removal occurred early in the morning and, according to the *New York Times*, cost "about $50,000."[16] Although it was originally sliced into three pieces and stored in a parking lot in Brooklyn, it was eventually shipped to a storage facility in Maryland.

Part of the reason *Tilted Arc* has been kept in storage for almost thirty years is because it cannot be sold. Although the *Tilted Arc* controversy did inspire the Visual Artists Rights Act (VARA), a law to protect the "moral rights" of visual artists (which, among other things, allows the artist to "prevent the use of his or her name as the author of the work of visual art in the event of a distortion, mutilation, or other modification of the work which would be prejudicial to his or her honor or reputation"), VARA applies only to works created during or after 1991[17] and therefore does not protect *Tilted Arc*.[18]

More practical concerns, however, will prevent the sale of *Tilted Arc*. What sane art collector or organization would purchase a sculpture that has been sliced into three sections, allowed to rot and flake for three decades, *and* has been disowned by its maker? The three pieces of COR-TEN steel that sit in a Maryland warehouse are no longer *Tilted Arc*; the physical components that were *Tilted Arc* are now rusting, worthless hulks.

In a confusing twist, however, GSA continued to pay tens of thousands of dollars for the upkeep of the pieces, shelling out almost $25,000 in 2005 to move them between government facilities in Maryland and more than $16,000 in 2008 to "stabilize" the decaying remains of *Tilted Arc*. This stabilization, which involves applying a waxy coating to the sections to keep them from rusting, must be repeated every three to five years at a cost of several thousand dollars for each application.

Until GSA decides to ship the steel slabs off to a junkyard, American taxpayers will continue to pay for a mistake made decades ago. Although Sen. William Proxmire (D.-Wisc.) wrote in 1976, "Where tax dollars are being spent, the public has a right to play art critic," the failures of both *Tilted Arc* and *Cedrus* show that the art that has been, and still is, created by the Art in Architecture program fails to appeal to the average citizen.[19] The same sort of elite art, familiar to the readership of *ARTnews*, the art critics of the *New York Times*, or the wealthy patrons of big-city art galleries, is still being paid for, to the tune of millions of dollars, by the Art in Architecture program. To understand how this still happens, it is important to know how the Art in Architecture program came into existence and how it now functions.

The Program's Background

As we have seen, the Great Depression–era art programs (the Public Works of Art Project, the Treasury Section of Fine Arts, the Treasury Relief Art Project, and the Federal Art Project) ended as America's involvement in the Second World War effectively eliminated the need for wide-scale subsidies to artists. In 1943 the Section of Fine Arts program ended, and for almost twenty years thereafter, there seems to have been no organized initiative for commissioning federally funded art work, although a number of art initiatives were formed and directed toward an international audience, some by the Department of State.

In 1962, however, Daniel Patrick Moynihan, then an assistant to the secretary of labor, wrote "The Guiding Principles for Federal Architecture," a series of recommendations to President John F. Kennedy on the topic of federal building construction. Among other things, he recommended that "where appropriate, fine art should be incorporated in the [building] designs, with emphasis on the work of living American artists."[20] A program was subsequently established within GSA to commission works of fine art for federal buildings and was named the Fine Arts program.

Funding for the program, which officially began in 1963, was provided by a percent-for-art scheme, with GSA reserving one-half of 1 percent of the estimated construction cost of federal buildings to purchase works of art to decorate that building. The Fine Arts program was soon shut down over concerns about the cost and public outcry regarding the quality of the commissioned art (particularly Robert Motherwell's *New England Elegy* in 1966), only to be revived by the Nixon administration in 1972 and renamed the Art in Architecture program in 1977.[21] After its revival, GSA began to partner with the National Endowment for the Arts (NEA) to select artists for Fine Arts commissions, with the NEA appointing art peers, handpicked "experts," to selection panels for Art in Architecture projects.

Through the 1970s, art commissioned by the GSA–NEA partnership continued to court controversy, with the bulk of commissions going to huge postmodern works. Pieces like George Sugarman's 1978 *Baltimore Federal*, an enormous, fanciful metal sculpture positioned in front of a federal courthouse, attracted criticism both on aesthetic fronts (a federal judge wrote to GSA asking rhetorically whether *Baltimore Federal* reflected the sobriety of the work being conducted within the building) and practical ones (community members voiced concerns that the structure would serve as a hiding place for muggers).

GSA reports that the piece was eventually "embraced" by the community, though exactly how they arrived at that conclusion is not mentioned. The controversy that erupted in 1981 over *Tilted Arc* shined a light on the flaws inherent in the GSA–NEA partnership. The drama that surrounded the piece, and the battle lines that formed over its removal, strongly suggests that the GSA–NEA collaboration, though supposedly choosing art *for* the public, was completely out of touch with the public's sensibilities.

In the aftermath of the *Tilted Arc* controversy, the Art in Architecture program underwent a series of changes. In *GSA Art in Architecture: Selected Artworks 1997–2008*, the program's adjustments after *Tilted Arc* are presented succinctly: "The GSA and NEA collaboration ended, and GSA assumed direct administration of the artist selection process. The Art in Architecture program implemented a new set of guidelines in 1991 that gave representatives of the local community, the client agency, and the GSA's regional administrators stronger roles in the selection of project artists."[22]

These changes reflect one of the chief battles of the *Tilted Arc* controversy, the battle between the desires of the artistic elites who testified on behalf of Serra and his art and, on the other side, the people who had to work around the piece and were footing the bill. Even though the GSA–NEA partnership was officially ended after the *Tilted Arc* debacle, the overreliance on "expert opinion" apparent in that selection process continues to plague the current Art in Architecture program. GSA's book insists that altering the selection process, "ha[s] helped the Art in Architecture program's commissions to become more responsive to . . . community needs and interests,"[23] but we can judge how much has really changed and whether any changes have resulted in the commissioning of more beautiful works of art.

The last point we consider before examining the procedures of the Art in Architecture program at present is its method of funding. The Art in Architecture program is a percent-for-art program. As is the case with the Eisenhower Memorial, funding for every new federal building (i.e., Art in Architecture project) must be approved by Congress. The program depends on voting legislators to either approve or ignore the funds earmarked for art projects in federal building budgets. There were a number of attempts in Congress to pass a law to permanently secure Art in Architecture funds in the late 1970s, but the issue seems to have fallen by the wayside for more than a decade afterward. In early 1993, though, the Art in Architecture program once more surfaced as a matter of discussion on Capitol Hill, albeit very briefly.

In May 1993, Sen. Jeff Bingaman (D.-N.M.) introduced the

"Art-in-Architecture Act of 1993." Bingaman's legislative record, both before and after the introduction of the bill, offers few hints as to why *he* would have introduced the bill, which sought to turn into law GSA's custom of allocating a percent of federal construction costs for art. The bill failed to leave the Senate, and no further bills on the subject were introduced. The identity of the cosponsor, however, answers many questions. The bill's cosponsor was Sen. Daniel Patrick Moynihan (D.-N.Y.), the same man who had written "The Guiding Principles for Federal Architecture" three decades earlier. Public works were Moynihan's passion, and he, not Bingaman, seems likely to have been the driving force behind the bill, but it is curious that he let the issue die with such little fuss.

After the bill was defeated, no changes were made to GSA's funding of Art in Architecture. One might have expected a fiscal conservative to seize upon the opportunity to introduce a bill restricting such spending, but no such bill appears in congressional records. The Art in Architecture program, then, seems to be floating in a sort of limbo state, tacitly approved by Congress but too unpopular to earn explicit support from it.[24]

Current Policies and Procedures of GSA's Art in Architecture Program

The *GSA Art in Architecture Policies and Procedures,* available through GSA's website, begins by listing the chief aims of the program: "The primary goals of the Art in Architecture Program," it reads, "are to commission *American* artists who are producing the *most critically esteemed and thought-provoking work of our era,* and to integrate their creative contributions in *meaningful ways* with an equally vibrant federal architecture" [emphasis mine].[25]

As the words emphasized in the sentence show, each Art in Architecture piece must, at minimum, check three boxes to satisfy the goals of the program. Each piece must be produced by an American artist (though "American" is later expanded to mean "citizens, Lawful Permanent Residents, or Permanent Workers of the United States") who is creating "the most critically esteemed and thought-provoking work of our era" (though no criteria are set forth as to *which critics* must hold the artist in high esteem, nor *which thoughts* the work ought to provoke) and, furthermore, the piece produced by this artist must be integrated in "meaningful ways" (again, "meaningful" is left open to interpretation) with the federal property on which it is housed.

The Art in Architecture program, then, could have either an incredibly difficult or an incredibly easy time meeting its own requirements, depending on the gloss given to words like *esteem* and *meaning*. In fact, in the absence of enough "critical esteem" for an artist, it doesn't seem implausible to suggest that GSA might manufacture more. In Judith Resnik and Dennis Curtis's *Representing Justice: Invention, Controversy, and Rights in City-States and Democratic Courtrooms*, the authors note that the "critical esteem" of completed GSA works is a matter of perspective, as "[several] commissioned works [have] garnered critical praise, albeit some of it derived from a circle of congratulation in which commissions awarded by the GSA receive citations from juries convened by the GSA."[26]

The selection process described in the *Policies and Procedures* document, the process instituted to democratize the art selection process after the failures of the GSA–NEA partnership, is a convoluted mess of bureaucracy.[27] In the *Policies and Procedures*, GSA breaks down the process into its own steps and stages, but we have done our best to simplify the collection of memos, offices, and proxy committees into a streamlined timeline for an Art in Architecture project, beginning with the idea for an art project and ending with a completed work of art.

Step 1: Internal Announcement, Planning, and Funding

GSA commissions art both for new federal buildings and for federal buildings undergoing substantial renovation. In the case of renovation, Art in Architecture funds may be used to conserve and restore older works of art rather than to commission new pieces. Once there has been an internal announcement of a new building or renovation project, the regional fine arts officer (RFAO), a Public Buildings Service (PBS) employee based in one of GSA's ten regions, works with the regional Portfolio Management Office (a PBS subdivision) and "other appropriate offices" to ensure that planning documents for the construction or renovation of a federal building include "appropriate funding, goals, and milestones for the Art in Architecture project." A Comprehensive Project Plan is created to address "all aspects of project management and acquisitions," and according to the Art in Architecture program's *Policies and Procedures*, "the acquisition of artists' services and their works of art will be included in that plan." The Office of Acquisition Management, in collaboration with the Design Excellence and the Arts Division, provides prototypical language for including Art in Architecture projects in the Comprehensive Project Plan.

Even before the project has been publicly announced, representatives of four distinct GSA offices or programs (Art in Architecture, regional Portfolio Management Office, Office of Acquisition Management, Design Excellence and the Arts Division) have had their say in planning the art for the new building or renovation.

Step 2: Building Design Contract Announcement

When the contract for lead designers and architecture/engineering teams is listed on FedBizOpps (the portal through which the federal government offers contracts), the RFAO is responsible for including the following information in the contract listing: "The lead designer will participate in GSA's established process for commissioning project artists and assist with the successful integration of their artworks into the architectural design, per the *GSA Art in Architecture Policies and Procedures*."[28] The lead designer chosen by GSA is automatically named as one of the members of the seven-person Art in Architecture Panel for the new building's artwork.

Step 3: Gathering the Panel

Once GSA chooses the lead designer and architecture/engineering team for the project, the Art in Architecture selection process begins in earnest. During the time between the selection of the design team and the official awarding of its contract, the regional commissioner (the head of the PBS for one of the ten GSA regions) and the Design Excellence and the Arts director (a national position within GSA) choose the rest of the project's panel members.

Each Art in Architecture panel consists of seven people: one GSA art peer from the PBS commissioner's National Register of Peer Professionals (a list of more than 650 private-sector design professionals), one art professional from the city or region of the building project, one federal client representative, one community representative, the regional commissioner's representative, the architect-engineer lead designer for the project, and the Art in Architecture program specialist.

No one may apply for a position on this panel. The Design Excellence and the Arts director appoints two of the members, the regional commissioner appoints three, the lead designer of the building, as previously noted, is obliged to participate, and the final member, the program specialist, is an Art in Architecture employee. The regional commissioner's representative is "usually the Regional Fine Arts Officer," so, in practice, at least two GSA employees sit on every panel. With the power to dictate exactly who sits on each panel, it is obvious that GSA has the power to garner consensus on art (via control over the selection of panel members) before the panels even meet.

The first meeting of the panel must occur "early in the project schedule, before the lead designer and architecture/engineering team have produced a design concept for the project."[29] The timing of this meeting exhibits the degree to which GSA desires artworks to be integrated into new buildings: the building design can't even be finalized before discussion about art begins. This merely emphasizes what was made obvious with the Eisenhower Memorial design "competition," that GSA is obsessed with awarding contracts based on reputation rather than choosing among completed, coherent designs.

Step 4: The Panel Meets

Once the panel is convened, the members are required to sign conflict-of-interest and nondisclosure forms; as we can see from the Eisenhower Memorial process, whether or not these forms perform their intended function is an open question. The *Policies and Procedures* document states that the program specialist and the RFAO are to begin the meeting

> by presenting to the Panel an illustrated overview of existing GSA building projects and art commissions. They will convey to the panel GSA's goal to commission the broadest possible spectrum of America's most talented artists, *and its mandate—as with federal architecture—not to endorse or promote an official or preferred style for art in federal buildings.* [emphasis mine] The Program Specialist and the RFAO will explain that the Art in Architecture Program has a national scope, and so artists who were born in and/or currently reside in the city or state where the building project is located will not be afforded preference in selection. The Program Specialist and the RFAO will show completed GSA art commissions as examples of artists' diverse approaches to federal commissions, and they will describe the steps the Panel will use to identify the best artists for the project.[30]

This presentation by the program specialist and the RFAO is a veritable conditioning exercise, one that tells the panel about the sort of artwork that GSA has historically commissioned, and, by extension, the sort of artwork that the panelists are expected to propose for the new commission. Though the panelists are told that GSA has no "official or preferred style for art," the illustrated overview of existing artwork surely conveys a sense of which styles are preferred.

Interestingly, some panels are also told that the commissioned art should be located in publicly accessible spaces. GSA, though, commissions artwork for buildings that are off limits to the general public, so it is unclear why this provision is sometimes included. The new Douglas A. Munro Coast Guard Headquarters Building in Washington, D.C., for example, is home to Art in Architecture art worth more than $2 million that is not accessible to the public.

After the rules and expectations for the Art in Architecture project are presented by the program specialist and the RFAO, the other members of the panel are given an opportunity to introduce themselves and their goals for the project, though the order in which the panelists may speak is prescribed by GSA. The *Policies and Procedures* document lists the introductions in the following order: lead designer, federal client representative, art professionals, and community representatives.

The lead designer is invited to articulate his or her design philosophy, discuss past collaborations with artists, and describe the ways he or she envisions working with artists on the commission. The federal client representative is then "asked to describe the function and uses of the proposed building, and to share any philosophical viewpoint (e.g., about the mission and history of the federal agency, or the role of the judiciary) that may aid the panel in its search for and review of artist candidates."[31] After the federal client representative, the panel's art professionals and community representative are permitted to speak about "the role of civic art, the identity of the project city and region, as well as the character of any local art community." The project manager (a regional GSA employee) will then outline the project's design milestones and projected construction schedule.

The sequential ordering of presentations is telling: before all else, GSA's desires are expressed by GSA employees, and *then* the GSA-appointed designer is invited to give a perspective on design. It is only after this that the wants and needs of the building's users are introduced, and only after *that* that members of the community in which the building will exist are brought in for discussion. The order of speakers may not give an explicit ranking of priorities or powers, but it absolutely suggests one.

After the introductions, the panel reviews the criteria used to evaluate artists for all GSA projects. The *Policies and Procedures* document states that the "panel will discuss the standards and weights that they recommend assigning to each of these criteria in evaluating artist candidates for this specific project. The program specialist and the RFAO will record the Panel's recommendations and report them to the project's Technical Evaluation Board."[32]

Step 5: Technical Evaluation Board Meeting

The Technical Evaluation Board (TEB) is the power behind the throne for Art in Architecture projects. After the first panel meeting, this board meets "to establish the relative weights of the selection criteria for the project, to conduct an initial screening of the Registry in order to establish the competitive field, and to conduct a technical evaluation that assesses the qualifications and past work of the short-listed project finalists."[33] The panel, then, makes *recommendations* about the relative weights and standards assigned to selection criteria, but it is the TEB that actually *decides* on the matter. Additionally, the scores that the TEB gives to short-listed finalists are *the* criteria that decide which artist gets the commission. Again, we find a mirror of this process in the method used to select Gehry as a designer for the Eisenhower Memorial, where a jury of designers and art critics made recommendations, but a separate panel had complete control over the final decision.

The TEB is entirely composed of GSA employees, with the RFAO, the program specialist, and the program manager (another Art in Architecture employee) all serving on it; the contracting officer (a regional GSA employee) is an advisory member. The TEB's composition is concerning, to say the least, and when one compares the powers of the TEB with those of the Art in Architecture Panel, the panel is clearly weaker in every respect.

At the first TEB meeting, the board members screen the artists currently on the National Artists Registry, a database of active artists, using the specific standards it has established for the project. Per the *Policies and Procedures* document, "The Selection Authority must approve the relative weights and standards established for the criteria before the selection process commences." The "selection authority" mentioned here is none other than the chief architect for GSA; he or she "serves as the Selection Authority for all Art in Architecture projects."[34]

Step 6: Project Announcement and Establishment of the Competitive Field

After the initial screening of the National Artists Registry, members of the panel (and, therefore, two of the TEB members) are invited to recommend artists for the project who are not yet on the registry, with the *Policies and Procedures* stating that "the Program Specialist will notify artists who are recommended by the Panel, but who are not yet on the Registry. These artists or their representatives must confirm the artists' interest in being considered for a commission and submit their materials to the Registry before the deadline posted in the FedBizOpps synopsis."[35]

GSA requires the panel to meet for the first time at least four weeks before the project's contracting officer posts a synopsis of the art project parameters on FedBizOpps. The synopsis, like all other documents and procedures in the Art in Architecture process, has very specific requirements: it must stay up for a minimum of thirty days, must provide information on how artists may be included in the National Artists Registry, and must also inform readers that only artists who are on the registry will be considered for the commission. In addition, the *Policies and*

Procedures notes that "the synopsis will list the technical criteria used to evaluate Registry artists for all GSA projects, and will state that the combined weight of these criteria is significantly more important than price."[36] Although it seems implausible that an artist who is not already known by a board or panel member and considered *en vogue* could have a real chance of receiving the commission, the public posting of the synopsis makes Art in Architecture commissions "open."

Step 7: Review of the Competitive Field

After the submission deadline for interested artists has passed, the panel reconvenes to review the portfolios of all artists in the competitive field. With the program specialist and the RFAO facilitating the discussion, the panel is required to recommend a short list of at least three artists for the TEB's final consideration. Each member of the panel must provide a written or verbal assessment of the short-listed artists in which the fitness of each finalist to the project is described. The facilitation by the program specialist and RFAO again raises red flags; given that both people (a) sit on the TEB, (b) may notify artists not yet on the registry of the commission opportunity, *and* (c) lead the discussion regarding a short list, it is clear that they wield an inordinate amount of influence over the artist selection process.

After the panel has produced a short list of artists, the program specialist or RFAO notifies the artists on that list and requests the submission of additional information to determine suitability. Per the *Policies and Procedures*, this information includes "a list of references (such as public art administrators or museum curators) the Program Specialist or the RFAO can contact to verify the artist's past performance on completed projects; a list of sales figures and/or commission budgets for the artist's completed projects; the artist's brief written statement of an overall approach to the GSA project; an explanation of how the artist's experience prepares him or her to accomplish the project; and the artist's statement that he or she can perform the work associated with the GSA commission within the identified budget."[37] As was noted at the beginning of this chapter with the *Cedrus* fiasco, no design is solicited at this stage by GSA. As bewildering as this sounds, given what we saw from the Eisenhower Memorial and what we know of the Design Excellence program, it is to be expected.

Once the TEB has received this information from the short-listed artists, it conducts both a technical and a price analysis for each artist. According to the *Policies and Procedures*, "The Board will determine an individual 'should-pay' price for each artist submitting proposals, and will assess each short-listed artist's documentation of his or her ability to produce an acceptable artwork for the GSA project budget and the determined 'should-pay' price ... The Board will use the recent sales figures and/or commission budgets to confirm whether the artist's proposal can be accomplished for the GSA project budget and the determined 'should-pay' price."[38] There is an obvious flaw in this step: the "should-pay" price is calculated from a chimera of reputation and previous sale prices; it is not a rigorous market estimate for a detailed design proposal. We can thus conclude that this step is essentially worthless and makes more apparent the emphasis placed on "trendy" or "fashionable" art attached to a name that was evident in the selection of a designer for the Eisenhower Memorial.

Step 8: Board Recommendation and Artist Approval

After completing both a technical evaluation and a price analysis for all short-listed artists, the TEB produces a report that contains "explanatory narratives and numerical or adjectival scores for each technical criterion (including Past Performance and Experience) as well as price evaluation for each artist and will incorporate the Art in Architecture Panel's assessments of the finalists." These scores are entirely subjective and, as such, are used more to mark out a preferred candidate than to identify the artist most fit for the commission. The report must also include "the Art in Architecture

Panel meeting minutes, the nondisclosure and conflict of interest forms, and the contracting officer's written concurrence that the Art in Architecture acquisition process has been followed."[39]

The TEB report must be approved by the Design Excellence and the Arts director before it is forwarded for regional review and approval. After gaining the approval of the regional commissioner, the RFAO then prepares a memo from the regional commissioner to the chief architect recommending approval of the board-selected artist.

After the chief architect approves the artist, a contract is developed for the project. The contract describes "the scope of services or work, roles and responsibilities, the sequence of tasks, schedules (including travel and meeting attendance), payments, and requirements for photographic documentation and maintenance instructions for the completed artwork." The contracting officer, the RFAO, and the artist discuss and negotiate the contract before it is signed.

Step 9: First Disbursement of Funds, Site Visit, and Preliminary Concept

According to GSA, funding for Art in Architecture projects has historically been allocated in two stages: a development allocation (one-quarter of the Art in Architecture budget) and a construction budget (three-quarters of the budget). The funding is allocated by congressional appropriation for the wider construction budget; as was noted in the previous section, there is no law obliging Congress to approve the art costs.

The project budget provides funds for a visit to the project site, an event that the *Policies and Procedures* document notes is intended to allow artists "to meet with representatives of GSA and the federal client agencies to learn about client-agency missions and to develop an understanding of the site's geography, history, and identity."[40] After the site visit, the artist must develop a preliminary concept that includes the project's "scope,

FIGURE 2.2 AN EXAMPLE OF THE ARTIST SCORES

SPENCER FINCH

Score	Criteria	Description
10	Media	Light / Sculpture / Architectural Arts. Many panelists thought that Finch's work could be integrated very successfully into the existing design of the new border station. Several panelists liked that much of Finch's work is immaterial (e.g., the effects of carefully calibrated light) and so would not create physical obstructions that might interfere with the operation of the port.
10	Content	Finch's work concerns the relationships among light, color, time and memory. Sometimes his work involves recreating in a new space the light from a different place and time. A major theme of his work is the tension between the objective nature of science and the subjectivity of perception. Panelists liked very much that his work deals with the relationships between places and movement through time a space, which would be thematically resonant with the border project.
9	Scope	National. Finch's work has been exhibited at several major venues for contemporary art around the nation, including the Whitney Museum in New York and Art Pace in San Antonio. See Background on page 19.
10	Materials	Stained glass / fluorescent lights / film gels. Finch uses ordinary, industrial materials to make his work. Panelists were unanimously impressed by Finch's ability to transform these unremarkable materials into stunningly beautiful and conceptually interesting artworks. Panelists also thought that Finch's materials could be easily integrated with the existing design of the port.
10	Style	Panelists thought that Finch's spare, industrial aesthetic would be a terrific match for the port architecture. Panelists thought that Finch's work was beautiful, engaging, and soothing. They also thought that because the work relies on light and color, it could be experienced more easily and fully in the busy port than an artwork that contained detailed imagery, text, or other elements that require close and deliberate scrutiny.
8	Experience, Past Performance, and Monetary Value	Finch has completed two public commissions and is working on a third. The budgets for his two completed commissions are smaller than the GSA commission, but panelists agreed Finch seemed experienced and ready to tackle something a bit larger. I. The Cave of Making, 2005, High Museum of Art, Atlanta, budget: $75,000. II. Atlantic Ocean (Sunrise), 2005, Bloomberg Building, New York City, budget: $70,000. III. 21/21 Design Sight museum (for 2007), Miyake Issey Foundation, Tokyo, Japan, budget: $30,000.

TOTAL SCORE: 9.50

Source: FOIA Online

William Caine, "Artist Evaluation — Spencer Finch"

design, location, size, material, color, texture, and all other aesthetic and material aspects of the work." This preliminary concept is developed alongside the lead designer and the regional project team.

Once the preliminary concept is completed, the RFAO and the program specialist receive a copy; after reviewing it with the contracting officer, the project manager, and the Design Excellence and the Arts director, the artist is advised on the acceptability of the concept.

It is important to note that the preliminary concept is intended *only* for internal GSA review; even the Art in Architecture Panel members who are not GSA employees are not permitted to view it. According to the *Policies and Procedures* document, "if the federal client requests a review of the artist's preliminary concept, the Program Specialist and the RFAO may consider these requests when the preliminary concept has been determined acceptable by GSA. In such instances, both the Program Specialist and the RFAO may present the preliminary concept to the federal client. The presentation will be in person, in order to ensure a full, clear, and accurate presentation of the artist's ideas and to address any of the client's questions about the preliminary concept."[41]

This provision is just another outrageous example of GSA's bureaucracy gone wild. Representatives of the federal client are not allowed to review the preliminary concept on their own but must instead receive a pitch from two GSA employees while looking at it; the artwork cannot simply be judged on its aesthetic merits. This procedure, whatever it is intended to do, looks coercive, and the withholding of the preliminary concept from the Art in Architecture Panel is equally suspect. If the Art in Architecture program weren't so concerned with hiring the fashionable artists du jour, no preliminary concept pitch to the federal client would be necessary; beautiful art requires no salesmanship to be seen as beautiful.

Optional Step: Peer Workshop

There is an optional step, or set of steps, that may occur after an artist has his or her preliminary concept approved. GSA may schedule a peer workshop, normally held at the artist's workshop, to "enhance the quality of the artwork." The workshop takes the form of a dialogue between the artist and other peer professionals and offers "expertise to the artist in areas such as design, fabrication, installation, maintenance, and conservation. Members of the PBS Commissioner's National Register of Peer Professionals will participate. At least one of the participants should be a peer knowledgeable in conservation issues to ensure that the proposed art materials are stable, durable, non-toxic, environmentally sound, and suitable for their proposed locations."[42] Either no such workshop occurred while Ursula von Rydingsvard was in the process of designing *Cedrus* or the "peer knowledgeable in conservation issues" dropped the ball. The *Policies and Procedures* document also notes that the regional office "may invite the federal client to attend the peer workshop"; it's likely this provision exists to reassure clients unhappy with the preliminary concept.

Step 10: Artist's Final Concept

After the acceptance of the preliminary concept, the artist is obliged to produce a final concept of sufficient quality to be exhibited publicly; unless explicitly stated otherwise in the artist's contract, the final concept becomes the property of GSA. Unlike with the preliminary concept, the final concept is presented to the panel by the artist. The *Policies and Procedures* document states that after the artist presents his or her final concept, "panel members will discuss the merits or drawbacks of the concept and make recommendations to GSA on whether fabrication and installation of the artwork should proceed. The RFAO and the Program Specialist will prepare minutes of the artist's final concept presentation meeting."[43]

Again, the panel's judgments are not decisive; the panel only provides recommendations. After the panel's recommendations are recorded, "the RFAO will incorporate the Panel's comments into a memorandum from the Regional Commissioner (or designee) to the Chief Architect, who authorizes the final approval of the artist's concept."[44]

Step 11: Second Disbursement of Funds, Fabrication, and Final Acceptance

Before fabrication and installation, the project manager recalculates the funds reserved for the project from the estimated construction cost. If the cost has risen substantially, the project manager, contracting officer, program specialist, and RFAO will determine if the artist will receive an increase in funding. After this calculation, the fabrication and installation commence. GSA aims for art projects to be installed before the official dedication of the building.

The artist is obliged to present to GSA "two identical sets of photographic documentation; information on fabrication, materials, and installation; and any special maintenance instructions for the fully installed artwork." In addition, the artist must also "provide a statement about the completed artwork that contains the artist's thoughts about the genesis, fabrication, installation, meaning and defining characteristics of the completed artwork, as well as any other details the artist can provide about the commission."[45] After a whirlwind of panels, meetings, and memos, a work of art is officially accepted by the federal government.

Summary

The steps just listed, it should be noted, are the *minimum* number of steps that it takes to commission an Art in Architecture project; any given project could take many more steps if short-listed artists withdraw, if multiple peer workshops are required, and so forth. When we consider the steps, and the participants, involved in the commissioning and creation of a piece of art, a number of points and themes jump out.

The roles of the RFAO and the Art in Architecture program specialist produce a sense of constant GSA control throughout all the project phases. The TEB, for example, seems to negate or make redundant the work of the panel (depending on whether the program specialist and RFAO are outvoted on the panel), and the TEB is, of course, nothing but a collection of GSA employees. Furthermore, the ability of the TEB and Art in Architecture Panel members to contact artists not on the National Artists Registry in order to get them *on* the registry is suspect; one might begin to get the idea that GSA has very clear ideas about the sort of art it wants.

Of course, the *sort* of art that is being produced is at the heart of the matter. The most "critically esteemed" art "of our era" is relentlessly postmodern, and its acclaim is fleeting. The celebrated works of one day are the laughingstocks of the next, and, in a bid to stay ahead of the curve, GSA commissions an inordinate amount of junk. The case studies that follow show just how consistently the Art in Architecture program misses the mark with its commissions.

Case Studies: The Best of the Worst

To give readers a sense of current Art in Architecture preferences, we selected our case studies only from works commissioned between 2006 and 2016. This decision meant that we immediately discarded more than thirty years' worth of GSA-commissioned artwork. We would be remiss, however, to avoid any mention of the anecdotes we uncovered from the preceding three decades.

Among other things, we found:

- The best-paid artist in the history of the Art in Architecture program is sculptor Tom Otterness. Otterness's works prior to receiving his Art in Architecture commissions included *Shot Dog Film* (1977), in which he adopted a dog from a Colorado animal shelter, tied the dog to a stake, and then filmed himself fatally shooting the dog. The Art in Architecture program was so appalled by Otterness's brazen disregard for life and animal cruelty laws that they awarded him almost $2.2 million in 2018 dollars to create whimsical and cartoonish sculptures to decorate federal courthouses.[46]

- Two of the most expensive pieces in Art in Architecture history, Martin Puryear's *Bearing Witness* (1997) and Keith Sonnier's *Route Zenith* (1997) (costing more than $1.5 million and $1 million in 2018 dollars, respectively) decorate the same building, the Ronald Reagan Building and International Trade Center in Washington, D.C. The construction of the building was plagued by delays and cost overruns, and when it finally opened in 1998, two years behind schedule, the total cost exceeded $1.2 billion. In 2015 GSA announced that the building, not yet twenty years after opening, needed "substantial" renovations.

- Many of the works that were "cutting edge" when commissioned now suffer from expensive, and entirely foreseeable, problems related to maintenance. Jim Campbell's aptly named *Broken Wall* (2005) has suffered cracks, *Hoe Down* (1979), an abstract work made of steel plates, has been damaged by children mistaking it for a deconstructed playground, and Christopher Sproat's *untitled*, a sculpture created in 1987 out of neon tubes, is so temperamental that a GSA employee wrote, "The lights break often due to their age. Replacements/repairs are becoming more difficult as few people are trained in cold cathodes and those who are are retiring . . . the rate of breaks and time of repair mean that almost constantly at least one tube [is] out, detracting from the intended look of the sculpture."[47] Indeed, when GSA set out to select an artist for another site, the San Ysidro Land Port of Entry in 2010, the panel explicitly rejected the work of a neon artist, saying the work "felt dated."

- Maintenance work on Art in Architecture pieces is not conducted solely by Art in Architecture employees. A significant portion of repair work is contracted out to companies such as McKay Lodge Fine Art Conservation Laboratory (whose owner, Robert Lodge, is a GSA art peer), who have received contracts totaling in the tens of millions to render "conservation services" to GSA.

- Although the removals of *Tilted Arc* and *Cedrus* garnered nationwide attention, other Art in Architecture works have been removed with less fanfare or have had campaigns organized to advocate for removal. Dimitri Hadzi's *Red Mountain* (1991) was removed from its original location (a courthouse in Birmingham, Ala.) in 2012 amid concerns about its ability to shield a potential attacker, concerns that are remarkably similar to those raised around George Sugarman's *Baltimore Federal* in 1978. Another piece, Guy Dill's *Hoe Down* (1979), was the subject of a *Tilted Arc*–style grassroots campaign for its removal from the front of a federal building in Huron, South Dakota.[48] Although the campaign was ultimately unsuccessful, a petition that was launched for the removal campaign in 1979 attracted more than 5,000 at a time when the population of Huron was around 13,000.

- Although most Art in Architecture commissions can be grouped into general categories such as sculpture, painting, and environmental art, we found two examples of Art in Architecture–commissioned *poetry*. In 1994 and 1997, American taxpayers paid for GSA to commission poems for buildings in New Jersey and Oregon, respectively, though it remains unclear how poetry can be meaningfully incorporated into federal buildings.

- Both Jim Sanborn and Larry Kirkland have received four Art in Architecture commissions apiece (when adjusted for inflation, each has received more than $1 million from GSA), and both have served on Art in Architecture panels. Kirkland is listed as a GSA art peer in panel documents; Sanborn is listed only as an artist representative. Their participation on the panels raises serious questions regarding potential and actual conflicts of interests.

Changes after the Approval of the Final Concept

The *GSA Art in Architecture Policies and Procedures* fails to mention any gap or steps between the approval of an artist's final concept and the fabrication of the work. From that document, one gets the impression that the "final" concept that is recommended by the panel and approved by the chief architect represents a hard-and-fast commitment by the artist. From our research of Art in Architecture panel documents and internal memos, however, we have found that designs can change dramatically even after the approval of the "final" concept. In the cases of Spencer Finch's *Glacial Erratic* (2014) and Buster Simpson's *Aerie* (2012), the final products do not remotely resemble the approved final concepts.

When Spencer Finch received a commission to create artwork for the Calais Land Port of Entry in Maine, he was chosen explicitly because of his ethereal use of light and color. He received perfect scores for both "Media" and "Content" in the technical evaluation, and it seems clear that the TEB had in mind an "immaterial" work, as the evaluation includes the comment, "Several panelists liked that much of Finch's work is immaterial (e.g. the effects of carefully calibrated light) and so would not create physical obstructions that might interfere with the operation of the port."[49]

The panel must have been surprised, then, when they were reconvened for the presentation of Finch's final concept and, instead of an "immaterial" work, Finch proposed a "field of wind-vanes on the triangular grassy area to the east of the port buildings."[50] The meeting notes are sparse, but it appears that only three of the panel members (one of whom was the Art in Architecture representative) expressed enthusiasm for the work; others raised questions about the fabrication of the wind vanes, and probably wondered how Finch had settled upon this idea. Given that Finch was explicitly picked for his usual brand of work, one can wonder why the panel didn't reject the proposal outright. There is no record in the meeting notes of the "unanimous enthusiasm" reported in the regional commissioner's memo to the chief architect recommending fabrication, but the concept was, nonetheless, approved for fabrication on September 12, 2007.

We do not have any further notes from the Art in Architecture program on the status of Finch's project, but we discovered that the wind vanes were installed, quickly damaged by the wind, and removed. The work that Finch created as a replacement, *Glacial Erratic*, is neither "immaterial" nor, in fact, anything like a "field of wind-vanes." *Glacial Erratic* is a collection of seven small drawings that depict the changing heat patterns on a rock outside of the Calais Land Port of Entry. There's no record of the panel being reconvened to approve this dramatic shift in design.

Equally befuddling is the end product of Buster Simpson's Art in Architecture commission in the state of Washington. Although much of Simpson's file was redacted by GSA, we are in possession of a description of Simpson's final concept, one that allows us to develop a clear mental image of the proposed sculpture:

> Buster Simpson explained that he wanted the artwork to reference the mission and work of the U.S. Army Corps of Engineers and respond to [the] site's location along the river . . . Buster Simpson's research efforts resulted in *Oxbow Auger*, a design concept for a kinetic artwork that combines ancient engineering tools with contemporary engineering innovations—the Archimedes screw (or water auger) and the helical wind rotor respectively. Buster Simpson

explained that the wind-activated sculpture is intended to tap into the water table. Water from the ground will run through the screw-like portion of the sculpture and irrigate the detention pond in which the artwork will sit. The flow of water from the sculpture will depend on wind speed.[51]

Simpson's sculpture, then, was supposed to be a dynamic work of art, one that included interactions with wind, water, and vegetation. Although the panel noted some concerns with the engineering of the project, the panel nonetheless recommended that GSA move forward with the project. The final panel meeting took place on June 15, 2011, yet the memo from the regional commissioner to the chief architect recommending fabrication was not written until May 30, 2012, and, in that memo, the work of art is not named as *Oxbow Auger* but rather as *Aerie*. Crucially, however, there is no mention that the artist's concept has changed; the regional commissioner's memo provides no description of the artwork. One can only imagine the surprise of the panel members, then, when GSA unveiled a static pyramid made up of twenty 360-pound limestone spheres. *Aerie* is devoid of any integration with water, air, or vegetation; it looks as if Simpson consciously fabricated the antithesis of the final concept approved by the panel.

As these two examples show, the end products of Art in Architecture commissions can differ dramatically from the final concepts approved by the panels. This discovery again raises the question of *why* Art in Architecture panels are convened; if the panel's role is, as we've begun to see, almost entirely ceremonial, who benefits from the panel's participation?

Site-Specific Art for a Nonexistent Site

It is fitting that this collection of case studies features an expensive, postmodern work of art created specifically for GSA's headquarters; it would be shocking if GSA decorated its main offices in any other way. Unlike other recent Art in Architecture commissions,

FIGURE 2.3   KITES, JACOB HASHIMOTO

Jacob Hashimoto, *Kites*, 2013, Sculpture

Source: Nicole Avila, U.S. General Services Administration, Fine Arts Collection

however, Jacob Hashimoto's *Kites* (2013) exists in a liminal space, neither fully on display nor fully hidden from the public eye. As strange as it may sound, GSA chose to commission a site-specific work for a site that did not yet exist and, by the current looks of things, may never.

Hashimoto's art, according to GSA documents, is inspired by traditional kite-making techniques and "combines the three-dimensional qualities of sculpture, such as volume and scale, with the flat, pictorial aspects of painting, operating as a hybrid of the two."[52] The abstract nature of Hashimoto's work is a familiar theme for Art in Architecture commissions. According to GSA, the abstract patterns printed on the miniature kites "can suggest any number of associations—including the diversity, complexity and interconnectedness of the critical work performed by GSA and the panoply of other federal agencies it serves."[53] Of course, because the abstract work merely suggests associations rather than having a definitive meaning, it can also suggest associations such as absurdity and waste.

Efforts to modernize the century-old GSA Administration Building kicked off in 2009. As a part of the renovations,

Hashimoto received a commission to create art for two planned atria. The east atrium has been completed, and half of Hashimoto's art installed, but the west atrium is, as of April 2018, nonexistent, so there is no telling when or if the second half of *Kites* will be put on display.

GSA's failure to complete the building and install Hashimoto's artwork aside, one must ask whether the hundreds of thousands of dollars paid to Hashimoto for *Kites* was money well spent at the GSA Administration Building. For all of its modern features and decorations, the building is plagued by window air conditioning units that pop out on all sides. These units are eyesores and create ugly stains on the stone beneath them; one can't help but think that the workers at the building would appreciate centralized air conditioning more than yet another postmodern artwork.

What Is That?

In a video posted to YouTube through GSA's official channel, Vesela Sretenović, senior curator of modern and contemporary art at the Phillips Collection in Washington, D.C., speaks about Andrea Zittel's *Planar Pavilion for the Denver Federal Center* (2014) in glowing terms, at one point going so far as to say that "there is nothing imposing or pretentious about the work."[54] To those who are not lovers of deconstructed, postmodern landscape art, however, *Planar Pavilion* appears to be both of those things. The rigid, inorganic structures rise abruptly from a gently sloping hill (hence it is imposing), and though it was commissioned as a work of art by the Art in Architecture program, one would forgive a lay observer for mistaking the installation for abandoned or half-built sheds (hence it is pretentious).

Planar Pavilion is an example of the "circle of congratulation" mentioned by Resnik and Curtis in *Representing Justice*; the piece was given a Design Excellence Award by GSA in 2016. Indeed, GSA touts the entire campus of the Denver Federal Center as a

FIGURE 2.4　PLANAR PAVILION FOR THE DENVER FEDERAL CENTER,
ANDREA ZITTEL

Source: Janet Paladino, U.S. General Services Administration,
Fine Arts Collection

Andrea Zittel, Planar Pavilion for the Denver Federal Center, 2014

progressive set-up, and it is mentioned on their website as a model
for future governmental facilities. The $599,054 piece of environ-
mental art is presented as one of many components at the complex
that is designed to cater to the "health and well-being" of both
employees and the general public. When one digs just beneath the
surface, however, it becomes apparent that the accessible face of
the site, one touted by GSA, is merely a façade.

Many of the pictures of *Planar Pavilion* posted to the Fine
Arts Collection website show groups of people doing yoga on
the platforms. GSA, then, is clearly trying to sell the piece as a
usable, accessible resource. Members of the public, however, only
have access to the Federal Center campus between 6:00 a.m. and
6:00 p.m. on weekdays; that is, when most people are in school
or working. Most members of the public, then, will never get to
"use" *Planar Pavilion.*

Even for employees, the artwork is less accessible than por-
trayed by GSA. *Planar Pavilion* lies well away from the nearest

building, meaning it is unlikely to be visited by the average worker on a short break. Supposing one did take a break long enough to visit the work, one might encounter another (entirely foreseeable) problem: snow.

In the video, Sretenović says that *Planar Pavilion* "functions in relation to the landscape and to the climate changes, so whether it is snowing or it's a sunny day, it reflects the environment in its own innate state."[55] Lakewood, Colorado, receives, on average, more than five feet of snow each year, and snow can be expected to fall in six months out of the year. It's difficult, then, to make sense of the word *functions* in Sretenović's statement; for half the year, it seems likely that the sculpture ceases to "function" at all.

"Public" Art behind Walls

The Douglas A. Munro Coast Guard Headquarters Building in Washington, D.C., houses three different Art in Architecture projects: *True Bearing* by An-My Lê (2013) (a series of photographs taken from "a neutral perspective that exposes the essential ambiguity of the medium of photography"), *Nocturnal (Navigation)* (2013) by Teresita Fernandez (a wall-mounted sculpture patterned after a navigational star chart), *Thanks from the Saved Ones* by Mark di Suvero (2013).

The average observer is not, however, permitted to view any of these works in person. All three of the works at the Douglas A. Munro Coast Guard Headquarters Building are included in the Art in Architecture program's rather condescendingly named "Out of Sight!" gallery, a collection of works that, though "held in trust for the American people," are inaccessible due to security concerns. Other works on this list include *Kryptos* (1990), an encoded sculpture at the Central Intelligence Agency Headquarters in Langley, Virginia.

Thanks from the Saved Ones is representative of di Suvero's general approach to art, as he has been creating large, abstract

FIGURE 2.5 THANKS FROM THE SAVED ONES

Source: Bill Caine, U.S. General Services Administration, Fine Arts Collection

Mark di Suvero, *Thanks from the Saved Ones*, 2013

sculptures outdoors since the 1960s. The sculpture is made of titanium and stainless steel and stands approximately twelve feet tall. The top portion of di Suvero's "boldly abstract" sculpture rotates, producing what GSA calls "ever-shifting sculptural silhouettes against the sky, trees and surrounding architecture," or what a typical observer might call "shadows."[56] *Thanks from the Saved Ones* is something of an oddity for an Art in Architecture piece, for although the *Policies and Procedures* document explicitly forbids the use of Art in Architecture funds for the creation of memorials, the name of the sculpture suggests a memorializing function. GSA appears to shy away from this notion, though, writing that the piece "might suggest any number of associations, such as jagged coastal rocks, billowing clouds and crashing waves."[57]

If we hold di Suvero's million-dollar sculpture to the requirement of "meaningful association" outlined in the *Policies and
Procedures*, it's difficult to ascertain how it fulfills it; an abstract
work of art that can "suggest any number of associations" while
endorsing none of them doesn't seem particularly meaningful.
For his own part, di Suvero (whose studio incubated a number
of avant-garde artists, including Ursula von Rydingsvard) claims
not to be an abstract artist, but says, rather, that he is a "corrupted
constructivist."[58] *Thanks from the Saved Ones* is the second piece
of art GSA has commissioned from di Suvero. He created *Motu*, a
four-story-tall "sculpture" made from COR-TEN steel and a rub-
ber tire, for the Gerald R. Ford Federal Building in Grand Rapids,
Michigan, in 1977.

Odds and Ends: Underwhelmed Panelists and "Unanimous" Agreement

Although GSA loves to conclude its panel notes by writing that
"unanimous" and "enthusiastic" approval has been given to a
final concept, we have found in our notes a number of examples
of panelists who have, in fact, expressed discontent. Consider, for
example, this epic rant by art peer Bruce Guenther at the final
concept proposal by artist Cliff Garten for a federal building in
San Francisco:

> Guenther said he thought the idea was marginal and the artwork
> will be viewed as decoration at best. Guenther said that he found
> the concept presentation to be pretentious and lacking conceptual
> rigor. He also said that he believes that Garten's concept will result
> in artwork that is mediocre and derivative. He explained that he did
> not vote for this artist at the artist selection meeting. Furthermore,
> he exclaimed, Garten is not a great American artist and that there
> is a reason why he doesn't exhibit his work in museums. Guenther
> commented that it was unfortunate that the site's rich history was
> not considered when Garten developed his concept—as there could
> have been some rich metaphors explored/created. Guenther said that

the artwork as proposed will be fine; the artwork won't interfere with ones [sic] enjoyment or experience of the building as it is likely that one won't notice it.[59]

Garten did, after the fact, revise his art concept after this outburst, but it still seems odd that GSA went ahead with commissioning an artist who its own art peer declared is "not a great American artist."

Likewise, when the panel for art at the new Los Angeles Federal Courthouse was presented with the final concept from Gary Simmons, panel members seemed less than impressed. Meeting minutes read, "Ms. Filer said that she is disappointed by Mr. Simmons' proposal. She said that it appeared to her that he had not spent much time working on its...Judge Morrow said that she agreed with Ms. Filer that it appears to her that Mr. Simmons has not devoted a lot of attention and time to the proposal. Kim Tachiki-Chin said that, to her, Mr. Simmons' proposal looks the same as his other paintings with stars."[60] Nonetheless, the memo to the chief architect says the panel was in "unanimous agreement to recommend" that the artwork be created.

One of the most interesting cases of an underwhelmed panel comes from the notes of Odili Donald Odita's final concept presentation meeting in Florida. Odita presented his concept to the panel, and then the panel deliberated. The meeting recorded an intriguing back and forth between a panelist and two GSA employees:

> Mr. Leivian accepts the artist's explanation for the gesture he is trying to make; however, the goal of the architecture was to minimize the grid and this concept doesn't do that...Mr. Leivian is new to the Art in Architecture program and was surprised that it doesn't require more than one concept to be presented. He would like to have options to consider. Architects prepare two or three designs or are fired are [sic] on the spot. Mr. Leivian asked if we are required to

take [the] concept presented or reject it. Ms. Entorf explained that GSA reviewed and approved the preliminary concept. After deliberation, the panel could recommend that GSA not accept the concept or make recommendations that the artist should address. Artists are selected for the work they do; however, they often respond in ways other than the panel expects…Ms. Baker pointed out that we can share panel feed back [*sic*] with [the] artist, but want to be careful to not to [*sic*] be too directive.[61]

Both Entorf and Baker are GSA employees, and the intent of their comments seems to be to discourage Leivian from sharing any pointed criticism with the artist. Leivian was not the only panelist to express dissatisfaction with the design, and yet only a few lines down from his exchange with the GSA employees one sees the following sentences: "All panel members accept the concept and feel it complements the building. They unanimously recommended that GSA approve the design."[62] Unless several panel members underwent dramatic and sudden changes of heart, the "agreement" to allow the concept to move forward cannot have been inspired by a feeling that the artwork "complements" the building. We have no way of knowing how (or even if) the dissenting panel members were convinced to allow the work to be created, but the Art in Architecture representative certainly seems to have discouraged the panel from engaging with the artist.

Conclusion

Despite the reforms that have taken place since the days of *Tilted Arc*, it's clear that the Art and Architecture program still has a transparency problem and a bias toward ephemeral art. Millions of dollars are still squandered each year on works of art that hardly anyone likes, and unless GSA shifts its focus from commissioning the most critically acclaimed art of the moment to commissioning artworks that the average citizen can both appreciate and be inspired by, it's almost inevitable that another fiasco will occur.

GSA must be reminded that it is not art critics to whom they must answer, but the American people, and the American people are best served by art that stands the test of time.

CHAPTER 3

The National Endowment for the Arts

A s the two previous chapters reveal, the messages that are communicated through federally funded works of art almost never support traditional ways of thinking about our history, identity, and values. The Eisenhower Memorial was deliberately designed to indicate a break with the rest of the National Mall, both in terms of aesthetic sensibility and, as Philip Kennicott was so quick to proclaim, in terms of how memorialization is framed. The Art in Architecture program's commitment to commissioning relentlessly postmodern art not only eschews traditional forms of art, but also shuns long-held ideas about the role and nature of beauty—and, in doing so, loses sight of beauty's Platonic associates, truth and goodness.

The National Endowment for the Arts (NEA), however, is perhaps the most notorious of all federal organizations involved in the creation of artwork. The controversies it generated with its funding choices were a major front in the culture wars of the 1990s, and new proposals for its elimination spring up every few years. As with the Eisenhower Memorial and the Art in Architecture program, it has cost American taxpayers an incredible amount of taxpayer money; unlike the other two, the lifetime bill for the NEA amounts to billions of dollars rather than millions.

When one mentions the NEA, it's natural to think also of its sister organization, the National Endowment for the Humanities (NEH). Like the NEA, the NEH has shown itself more than capable of awarding perplexing grants. In recent years, the NEH has seen fit to fund a book-length study of the history of French lesbian activism since World War II, a project to investigate the Golden Age of Podcasting (how long, one wonders, was this particular epoch?), and a video game based on Henry David Thoreau's *Walden*. The commitment to head-over-heels activism that is detectable in NEA grants, however, is unmatched by anything put out by the NEH or even the Art in Architecture program. A cursory scan of recent NEA grants reveals an array of bewildering projects.

One recent noteworthy NEA grant is the $20,000 that was awarded to the San Francisco Mime Troupe in 2017 to produce *WALLS*. The NEA's grant entry describes *WALLS* as a "satirical new musical theatre work" that explores "immigration, gun violence, depression, the public education system, and racial tensions." The entry on the San Francisco Mime Troupe's website goes into more detail:

> *WALLS* asks the question: How can a nation of immigrants declare war on immigration? The answer: FEAR! L. Mary Jones (Velina Brown) knows all about fear. As a top agent for I.C.E.—Immigration and Customs Enforcement—she knows how to stoke fear to keep her country safe. Fear of people like Bahdoon Samakab (Rotimi Agbabiaka), a Somali refugee escaping oppression, fear of Cliodhna Aghabullogue (Lizzie Calogero), an Irish woman yearning to be American, and fear of Zaniyah Nahuatl (Marilet Martinez), whose family comes from . . . here. As a foreigner in a land her people have worked for thousands of years suddenly Zaniyah is a criminal, an

illegal, a "bad hombre." What part of herself will this American give up to pass as "American?" Will she? Can she? Should she? Can someone leave part of themselves behind without losing their mind? And is it better or worse that she crossed the border to find Agent L. Mary Jones—the woman she loves?[1]

This "work of art" that the NEA chose to fund is difficult to distinguish from outright propaganda; it was clearly the intention of the writers to make a provocative statement on just about every hot-button social and political issue in the contemporary United States. In this absurd work of political theater, those who disagree with the writers and performers on issues from immigration to identity are ridiculed. The San Francisco Mime Troupe takes as its targets many of the same taxpayers whose money it has accepted.

If *WALLS* were alone among suspect recipients of NEA patronage, it might be easy enough to pass over as an anomaly, but a quick scan of works awarded NEA funds (both directly and through subsidiary organizations) reveals countless other grants of questionable merit and multiple ways to channel federal funds to controversial artists. Some works, such as *WALLS*, are explicitly political; others, such as choreographer Ann Carlson's *Doggie Hamlet*, a piece of "performance art" in which "five performers, three herding dogs, a dog handler, a dog trainer and a flock of sheep" chase each other around a pasture, are merely absurd wastes of taxpayer funds.[2] To makes sense of the NEA's suspect funding choices, we must take a look at its history, the structure it has adopted, the relationships it has formed with other organizations, and the priorities it has made evident throughout its existence.

The Program's Background

The NEA and the NEH came into being in the mid-1960s, just two of the many domestic programs to emerge from President Lyndon Johnson's Great Society initiative. After signing off on the

National Endowment on the Arts and the Humanities Act of 1965 in September 1965,[3] Johnson said, "Art is a nation's most precious heritage. For it is in our works of art that we reveal to ourselves, and to others, the inner vision which guides us as a Nation. And where there is no vision, the people perish."[4] President Johnson's insightful comment about art and vision makes one wonder if he foresaw some of the problems that would arise to plague federal art organizations. Indeed, were Johnson able to see the current state of NEA, he might well ask if its vision has anything to do with the priorities and concerns of the people for whom it was intended; it's hard to imagine that many citizens would look at the projects currently receiving NEA grants and see our "nation's most precious heritage."

Although the NEH initially received a larger appropriation from Congress ($5.5 million in 1966 compared to the NEA's $2.5 million[5]), the NEA grew at a faster clip and eventually attracted more attention. This attention was generated chiefly from the NEA's funding, even at that embryonic stage, of nontraditional artists. As is recounted in the NEA's publication *National Endowment for the Arts: A History, 1965–2008*, "In the visual arts the agency supported pop art and neo-surrealism, while at the same time it fostered appreciation of other styles and genres. The Arts Endowment did not reward only established artists; it encouraged young and fresh talents previously overlooked or growing in acceptance...front-line figures in the historic roster of 1967 visual arts grantees included Leon Polk Smith, Mark di Suvero, Dan Flavin, Donald Judd, Manuel Neri, Tony Smith, and H. C. Westermann. None of these artists were traditionalists."[6] Interestingly, Flavin, Neri, T. Smith, and di Suvero have all received commissions from the General Services Administration's Art in Architecture program in addition to their grants from the NEA.

Considerable overlap in artists whose work has been supported by the Art in Architecture program and the NEA should not come as a surprise; from its inception, the NEA cultivated an intimate relationship with the General Services Administration (GSA). In the early 1970s, for example, the NEA and GSA worked together to host a series of federal design workshops; in doing so, they appear to have regarded each other as equals. After public backlash to early Art in Architecture commissions, including the previously mentioned attempt by townspeople in South Dakota to remove Guy Dill's *Hoe Down*, however, the dynamic between the two organizations changed. To prevent further controversies, the NEA took the reins of the Art in Architecture program, and, for a period, the three-person panels that made commission selections for the Art in Architecture program were made up entirely of the NEA's "experts." The *Tilted Arc* debacle, however, came under the NEA's regency and led to control of the Art in Architecture panel shifting back into the hands of GSA, where it has stayed.

While the NEA was in charge of commissioning artists for the Art in Architecture program, it also ran its own program for the creation of public art. The Art in Public Places program, which ran from 1967 to 1995, was not so different from the modern Art in Architecture program insofar as it awarded funds to artists without requiring them to submit detailed design concepts. According to Ronald Lee Fleming, the program "offered grants to artists and arts organizations to create works of their own design without giving specific guidelines for the art's creation as a commissioning agency would have. And unsurprisingly, given the artistic mores of the day, many of the APP's early public artworks were abstract sculpture."[7] The Art in Public Places program, then, was simply handing over taxpayer dollars to artists without mandating specific guidelines for the creation of artwork, eager to see what would be made. The naïveté displayed by the NEA in organizing (or, more accurately, *not* organizing) this program is scandalous.

This program, which produced more than seven hundred works during its run, often ended up giving funds to support the purchase of artworks from artists who had already received individual-artist fellowships from the NEA.[8] A notable example of an Art in Public Places artwork is Alexander Calder's *La Grande Vitesse* (1969). An abstract artist whose other public artworks include the hideous *Mountains and Clouds* (1986) in the atrium of the Hart Senate Office Building in Washington and the GSA-funded *Flamingo* (1974) in Chicago, Calder created *La Grande Vitesse* in his studio in France, then brought it over to be installed on a plaza in Grand Rapids, Michigan.

From the beginning, this work attracted controversy, and it remains a point of contention among citizens of Grand Rapids to this day. A 2013 MLive article quoted one *Grand Rapids Press* reader as saying, "I've felt from the beginning that this is a useless piece of junk and an eyesore."[9] The plaza where it sits has been described as "stark" and "windswept," and though the Calder piece has its defenders, many residents still likely agree with this sentiment expressed by a critic in 1969: "After Calder gets his (money) and goes back to France, some evening he'll be sitting in some pub and saying, 'Boy, did I hoodwink those guys over in Grand Rapids.'"[10] Calder's response to the criticism expressed by Grand Rapids residents does nothing to discourage that impression, as he is recorded as saying, "If they don't like it, leave it alone."[11] The public space, as far as Calder was concerned, belonged to *La Grande Vitesse*, whether or not the people of Grand Rapids liked it.

Although the Art in Public Places program produced its share of controversies during its thirty-year run, it was the NEA's individual fellowships and grants that raised the most suspicion among conservatives around the country and on Capitol Hill. As with the Art in Public Places program, many of the individual fellowships and grants funded by the NEA were for artists in emerging styles. This trend raised concerns among legislators from the first years of the Endowment, as "some legislators expressed anxiety that the NEA would escape federal oversight, as well as bypass the cultural norms of the American majority. Others saw money for new styles in art as a form of state censorship of more

FIGURE 3.1   LA GRANDE VITESSE

Source: Wikimedia Commons

Alexander Calder, *La Grande Vitesse*, Sculpture, installed in Grand Rapids, Michigan, in 1969

traditional styles."[12] That the art funded by the NEA could end up out of step with the "inner vision" of the vast majority of American citizens, is, as we have seen, a perennial concern.

Anxieties about the role and reach of the Endowment simmered throughout the late 1960s and Seventies, but, for the most part, did not boil over. As the Eighties became the Nineties, however, critics began to find concrete works on which to attach some of their fears and, later, outrage. Ironically enough, the artists who incited the great backlash against the NEA in the 1990s did not receive direct artist grants from the NEA, but, instead, received federal funds indirectly. Andres Serrano's *Piss Christ* (1987) and Robert Mapplethorpe's retrospective *Robert Mapplethorpe: The Perfect Moment* (1988) changed how the NEA does business, and almost drove it to extinction.

As the name implies, the sixty-by-forty-inch Cibachrome print of Serrano's photograph shows a plastic crucifix submerged in what the artist alleged was his own urine. While the content of Serrano's picture could have sparked a public debate on its own, it was the money and praise that he received *after* creating it that generated the real controversy. In 1988, he was awarded a $15,000 fellowship by the Southeastern Center for Contemporary Art (SECCA) as a part of their Awards in the Visual Arts program, and the SECCA was able to offer those fellowships because of the funding it received from the Equitable Life Assurance Society, the Rockefeller Foundation, and, last, but certainly not least, the NEA.[13] The recipients of the Awards in the Visual Arts had their works included in a traveling exhibition; after some of Serrano's works, including *Piss Christ*, were exhibited at the Virginia Museum of Fine Arts, complaints began to roll in.

Around the time that *Piss Christ* was beginning to attract widespread negative attention, the recently deceased Mapplethorpe's touring retrospective, *The Perfect Moment*, was due to arrive in Washington, D.C. The Institute of Contemporary Art (ICA) at the University of Pennsylvania had been awarded NEA funds to support the exhibition, but when the time came for the show to go up in the Corcoran Gallery of Art in Washington, D.C., the museum backed out. The reason for their withdrawal was the inclusion in the exhibition of a series of explicitly sexual photographs, including a self-portrait of Mapplethorpe with a bullwhip inserted in his anus. With the Corcoran unwilling to host the show, the exhibition went instead to the Washington Project for the Arts, where it attracted large crowds.

Conservatives demanded that the NEA face reprisals for its role in providing funding to both Serrano and Mapplethorpe's exhibits, and a bill to reduce the NEA budget by $45,000 (representing the $15,000 Serrano received from SECCA and the $30,000 that had been awarded to ICA for *The Perfect Moment*) quickly passed in the House. While the NEA's budget wasn't substantially reduced that year, the ire of conservative congressional representatives had been raised and would not abate any time soon.

While the tensions raised by Serrano and Mapplethorpe simmered, a group of artists who felt that they had been wronged by the NEA forced the Endowment back into a defensive stance. Karen Finley, Tim Miller, John Fleck, and Holly Hughes had all passed the peer-review process for NEA grants and were recommended for grants, but NEA chief John Frohnmayer vetoed each of their grants for explicitly content-based reasons. Finley, for example, was known for her "feminist performance art," which often took the form of the auteur stripping naked and pouring chocolate on herself. In a case that went all the way to the Supreme Court, the "NEA Four" were eventually awarded grants of an equal amount to those they had been denied. By the time of the lower court judgment for the NEA Four in 1993, however, the damage had been done. Public and governmental opinion was fast swinging against individual-artist grants.

By the mid-1990s, the Republican Party had declared war on the NEA. Opposition to the NEA became a significant piece of the GOP platform in the lead up to the 1994 congressional elections, with the Republican "Contract with America" calling for the outright elimination of the NEA.[14] The NEA, of course, lived on, but it was forced to make some large concessions in order to survive. The NEA ended its practice of offering individual grants to visual artists, though creative writers and translators could still receive direct grants.

The fight against the NEA wasn't merely a reaction to obscenity, though it's impossible to deny that the funds that went to Serrano and Mapplethorpe's exhibitions set off the chain of events that led to the end of individual grants. It was equally about fears of corruption and elitism in the world of federally funded artwork, fears, as Newt Gingrich put it, that self-selected elites were using "tax money to pay off their friends."[15] Federal funding for the arts, critics like Gingrich claimed, amounted to little more than welfare for the rich, and, with the end of individual-artist grants, one source of that welfare had been cut off.

In theory, then, the NEA that exists today should be markedly different from the NEA that was founded in 1965. The hands-off approach that allowed an NEA employee active during the Art in Public Places program years to say "If you believe in what individual artists can do, stand back and let them do it" should no longer be detectable.[16] How such a hands-off approach was tolerated in the realm of public art—and therefore public funding—for so long is a mystery in and of itself, but ongoing projects like *WALLS* and *Doggie Hamlet* raise the question, Have things really changed as much as the NEA would like the public to believe? On its website, the NEA acknowledges that it is no longer able to fund individual artists, but it follows up this admission with a caveat: "We encourage applicant organizations to involve individual artists in all possible ways."[17] The implications of the phrase "in all possible ways" are troubling; it could be the case that the organization has abided by changes in the letter of the law without embracing the spirit.

The NEA at Present

The Endowments' unique funding arrangements offer one avenue for obeying the letter of the law and ignoring the spirit. One of the chief differences between the present Endowments and the Art in Architecture program lies in how they receive their funding.

Funding for the Art in Architecture program is specific to each project, with the money for every new artwork taken from the site's building or restoration budget. The NEA and NEH, in contrast, are explicitly allocated funds (budget lines) in the annual congressional budget, and this funding is many times the size of what is spent by the Art in Architecture program, or even the Eisenhower Memorial, in any given year. Not all of this money stays with the Endowments, however.

The NEA and NEH are required to distribute a significant portion of their yearly allotments to regional and state councils that are then able to make grants of their own. Ideally this chain of grants allows the lower-level organizations to better address concerns in specific communities. The NEA is required to distribute at least $200,000 to art councils in all fifty states (though in practice it gives much more); it also supports six territory art councils (the Northern Marianas are not currently eligible for funding, though they have received it in the past)[18] and six regional art councils. In 2017 it distributed a total of $49,043,255 to the state, territory, and regional art councils, with each state receiving at least $618,000 and each regional council receiving between $1,075,000 and $1,667,700. States receiving NEA funding must match the funds 1:1 with state governmental funds (there are cases, though, where the art council had not been appropriated funds by the state yet still received federal funding, as occurred in Illinois in 2017),[19] while the regional arts organizations are permitted to make use of both public and private funds to match NEA disbursements. The NEH, by way of contrast, provides general operating support to state and jurisdictional humanities councils on an annual basis. NEH grants are awarded on a five-year timeline: three years within which the grant provides funding, and two years within which the grant must be closed out.

The state and regional art councils aren't required to play by the same set of rules stipulated for the Endowments; they are able to do things that would be unthinkable on the national level. The

Indiana Arts Council, for example, awards individual-artist grants. The grants awarded for FY 2018 include the vague ($2,000 for a novel whose one-line description notes only that it will feature "an autistic main character"), the suspect ($2,000 for a "week-long driving trip" in order to write "authentically" about the setting for a novel; $1,400 for a five-day stay at an "artist's retreat"), and the bizarre ($2,000 for a brass band composition about a road that runs "past junkyards, a Latino body shop, rusted train cars, abandoned homes and pastures").[20] By and large, however, the state arts councils do not appear to have taken up the cause of individual-artist grants; only a few states still offer them.

The regional arts organizations (RAO), however, appear to be far more complicated, both on the topic of individual-artist support and in their general operations. The six RAOs did not emerge as a block, but, instead, came into being in the 1960s and 1970s to facilitate art programming efforts among the states. Arts Midwest, the Mid-America Arts Alliance, the Mid Atlantic Arts Foundation, the New England Foundation for the Arts, South Arts, and WESTAF all operate independently of one another, but all share an emphasis on promoting touring artists and reaching underserved communities. While each of the RAOs offers some degree of support to individual artists, only the Mid-America Arts Alliance explicitly offers individual artists grants for the creation of new work; the other RAOs, probably in an effort to avoid criticism over a controversial work, offer artists "creative fellowship retreats" and "community building" projects rather than money without restriction.

Curiously, however, even though the Mid Atlantic Arts Foundation itself does not offer individual-artist grants, it administers individual-artist grants for the states of Delaware, Maryland, and New Jersey and provides more than $500,000 in individual-artist support each year.[21] It is an odd arrangement, one surely defended by arts bureaucrats on the grounds of expediency and "getting the most bang for the buck," but it nonetheless is peculiar that three states receive NEA funds and then promptly turn them over to a regional agency (that has also received NEA funds) to be disbursed to individual artists. If the point of the NEA's distribution of funding to the states is to address local concerns, what good is it for that money to be managed by a nonlocal agency?

Returning to the conditions of RAO funding, note that these organizations must collect matching funds from both public and private sources. In researching the sources of funding, one comes across several curious sources, but none more surprising than a recent donor to the New England Foundation for the Arts: the Embassy of the United States in Islamabad, Pakistan. According to the NEFA website, the embassy donated an amount in excess of $100,000 sometime since June 2017.[22] Why that embassy felt compelled to donate such a sum to an arts organization halfway around the world is unclear, but the donation from the embassy in Islamabad is not its first questionable decision regarding art. In 2014 multiple news outlets reported that the Department of State was planning to spend $400,000 on a work of art by John Baldessari for the embassy in Islamabad, a decision they justified in a memo by saying, "This artist's product is uniquely qualified. Public art which will be presented in the new embassy should reflect the values of a predominantly Islamic country."[23] What was this artwork? An almost nine-foot-tall polyurethane camel "contemplating" a more-than-ten-foot-tall needle. The records are unclear as to whether the embassy went through with the purchase after the public backlash.

While the state and regional organizations can directly award grants to visual artists, the NEA can only provide funds to visual artists indirectly. Studios and museums may apply for NEA funds to host exhibitions by specific visual artists and support the creation of artwork by specific artists. For example, in 2017 $10,000 was awarded to 29 Pieces in Dallas, Texas, to "support the creation of a public art work inspired by different world traditions. The project's goals are to encourage audiences to reflect on civic unity and peace, as well as their own personal well-being, in relation to the contemporary challenges and discord plaguing our urban landscape."[24] The description of the artwork would not seem out of place in any Art in Architecture release. The grant description, however, is quick to point out that the "project will involve two dozen Dallas public high school students who will work under master artists to construct fiberglass and mosaic sculptures," thus portraying it as a sort of community-bonding effort, before concluding by noting that "participating artists will include Darryl Ratcliff and Vicki Meek." The grant request from 29 Pieces, then, reads almost as a conditional contract, as if that organization had already signed an agreement to commission an artwork contingent on the NEA agreeing to hand over the funds. This type of grant is not unusual among recent NEA awards, and it certainly gives the impression that the NEA has simply moved from funding individual artists to funding art patrons.

The NEA can also funnel money to visual artists through another class of grants, one that falls under the banner of "place-making." Placemaking grants have gone to cities to support artists' incubators and festivals, but they may also be used to fund the purchase of particular artworks if a city can make the case that those artworks will act as a catalyst for community development. The city of Wilson, North Carolina, for example, has received more than $1 million from the NEA to support the creation of a "Whirligig Park," a two-acre park featuring massive kinetic sculptures made out of trash.[25] Created by a local artist named Vollis Simpson, the city of Wilson has received grants from the NEA's "Our Town," "Access to Artistic Excellence," and "Art Works" initiatives to restore and relocate the highway signs, HVAC fans, bicycle parts, and other eclectic components that make up the whirligigs.

The Our Town initiative, in particular, is intended to support projects that attempt to leverage artistic and cultural assets into spurs for economic development. The artwork, in theory, attracts public attention, which in turn attracts developers, business owners, and new residents to a previously undesirable area. In the

FIGURE 3.2   WHIRLIGIG PARK

Source: Wikimedia Commons

Simpson's whirligigs high in the air at the future Vollis Simpson Whirligig Park

description for one of the grants awarded to the city of Wilson, the NEA states that the Whirligig Park has already contributed "to the economic, social, and physical revitalization of the community."

Although the Our Town initiative proclaims that public art installations can have a positive economic impact on towns and cities, it seems to sidestep the crucial question of "fitness." An ugly work of art, or a beautiful work of art in the wrong place, is unlikely to serve as a catalyst for revitalization, and in the case of Wilson, it seems far more likely that Whirligig Park is the former rather than the latter. While the Whirligig Park project, for example, has received glowing reviews in the press, some online reviews of the site by locals are more muted. One Wilson resident called the park "a little ridiculous and sad," while another said that it's "nothing to brag about."[26]

The Arts and Artifacts Indemnity Program

Even though questionable projects like the Whirligig Park are still funded by the NEA, the most alarming program that exists in the modern NEA is not explicitly connected to avant-garde or controversial works of art. In fact, many of the works covered by this program are indisputably beautiful works of art. But the Arts and Artifacts Indemnity program puts the American taxpayer in a very dangerous position while rewarding cash-rich museums; as such, it needs to be brought under the microscope.

The NEA is the administrator for the Arts and Artifacts Indemnity program, but the Federal Council on the Arts and Humanities (made up of a host of government notables, including the heads of the NEA and the NEH) is the nominal head of the program. The program provides indemnity to museums "planning temporary exhibits that involve bringing works of art and/or artifacts from abroad to the United States or sending works of art and/or artifacts from the United States abroad."[27] The purpose of this program is to minimize the costs of insurance for such temporary exhibitions, although the costs of insuring these exhibitions are not prohibitively high for the incredibly wealthy institutions that benefit from the program's work.

When an exhibit is approved under the Arts and Artifacts Indemnity program, it is "backed by the full faith and credit of the United States. In the event of loss or damage to an indemnified object, the Federal Council must certify the validity of the claim and request Congress to authorize payment."[28] Although this program might initially strike one as innocuous, the prospect of "loss or damage to an indemnified object" brings us to the threat taxpayers face: exposure.

With a change approved by Congress in 2014, American taxpayers face exposure up to $22.5 billion at any one time under the Arts and Artifacts Indemnity program, with any one international exhibition able to be indemnified for $1.8 billion and any domestic exhibition for $1 billion. Those are staggering numbers, and it goes without saying that most taxpayers are unaware that they could be on the hook for billions of dollars for art exhibitions that most have never heard of, let alone seen.

Who benefits from this arrangement? Certainly not the taxpayer. Some of the wealthiest and most prestigious museums in this country, however, benefit a great deal from the Art and Artifacts Indemnity program. Combined with support grants from the NEA and NEH, some museums are able to indemnify exhibits for almost nothing. Consider the deductible scale for exhibitions provided on the Art and Artifacts Indemnity program website:

1. $15,000 deductible for exhibitions up to $2 million in indemnified value;
2. $25,000 deductible for exhibitions over $2 million up to $10 million in indemnified value;
3. $50,000 deductible for exhibitions over $10 million up to $125 million in indemnified value;
4. $100,000 deductible for exhibitions over $125 million up to $200 million in indemnified value;
5. $200,000 deductible for exhibitions over $200 million up to $300 million in indemnified value;
6. $300,000 deductible for exhibitions over $300 million up to $400 million in indemnified value;
7. $400,000 deductible for exhibitions over $400 million up to $500 million in indemnified value;
8. $500,000 deductible for exhibitions over $500 million in indemnified value.[29]

As astonishing as it may seem, under the Arts and Artifacts Indemnity program, the deductible a museum must pay for coverage could almost never exceed more than 1 percent of the total value of the exhibition; that is, the total sum the American people would have to pay in the case of damage. When museums benefit from both the Indemnity program and other sources of federal funding, however, the situation goes from absurd to downright ludicrous.

In late 2016, for example, the Walters Art Museum in Baltimore hosted *A Feast for the Senses: Art and Experience in Medieval*

Europe, and that exhibition received indemnity coverage totaling $60,113,290.[30] Using the scale provided by the Arts and Artifacts Indemnity program, we know that the Walters paid a $50,000 deductible for that coverage, amounting to less than one-tenth of 1 percent of the exhibition's appraised value. Interestingly enough, that exhibition received support from *both* the NEA and NEH, and that support *exceeded* $50,000 ($45,000 from the NEA; $300,000 from the NEH under the title of *A Sense of Beauty: Medieval Art and the Five Senses*).[31] This means that if the exhibition at the Walters had been damaged, the museum would not have been any worse off than they had been before receiving the Endowment grants; the American taxpayers would have had to cough up millions, but the museum wouldn't have owed anything. The Art in Architecture program was beset by a ridiculous "circle of congratulation," but the circular flow of money between the Endowments and rich institutions might be more unbelievable.

Examples can be found of similar patterns across the country, where museums have received both grants (either from one of the Endowments or from a state-level organization) and indemnity from the federal government. One could justifiably ask whether the Walters Art Museum or the Museum of Fine Arts in Boston really need the federal assistance (both in the form of grants and indemnity) that they have received, or whether the Arts and Artifacts Indemnity program really just constitutes welfare for the rich. The NEA of the present is a different beast than the NEA of the past, and, to be sure, it has made some positive changes, but it continues to channel funds to controversial projects. Now, as the administrator of the Arts and Artifacts Indemnity Program, it puts taxpayers on the hook for billions of dollars to save museums from putting their own funds at risk.

Summary

The federally funded works that we have reviewed, and the processes that produced them, are simply not good enough for the American people. The Art in Architecture program and the Endowments, however, have existed for more than fifty years and have weathered their share of storms and calls for dissolution. Even with trails of awful artwork in their wakes and track records of dubious practices, they're not going anywhere. Our efforts must go to reform, to preventing the same mistakes of the past from happening again. The murky waters of the Swamp have served as cover for art programs for decades, but now, with some glimmer of light having been shone on the inner workings of the Eisenhower Memorial Commission, the Art in Architecture program, and the NEA, we can begin to demand that our art be created through fair and open commissioning processes, that wasteful spending be reined in, and that the art that is created reflects our national values. The cost of inaction is steep. The federal programs breed copycat programs at the state and local levels; unless we demand change, it's virtually guaranteed that the art with which we are surrounded will begin to shape us, and our descendants, in ways we do not want.

Art in Architecture
Commissioned Artwork Data

This data set includes original price and adjusted price for every known Art in Architecture work produced between 1975 and 2016.[1] Adjusted prices were calculated using inflation rates as of March 14, 2017.

Year	Artist	Title	Classification	Unadjusted Cost	Inflation Multiplier	Adjusted Cost	Adjusted Annual Total
1975	Duayne Hatchett	Equilateral Six	Sculpture	$45,000	4.528	$203,760.00	$1,037,591.20
1975	Robert Maki	Trapezoid E	Sculpture	$20,000	4.528	$90,560.00	
1975	Isamu Noguchi	Landscapes of Time	Environmental art	$100,000	4.528	$452,800.00	
1975	John W. Queen	Tribute to the American Soldier	Sculpture	$15,000	4.528	$67,920.00	
1975	Frank Stella	Joatinga	Sculpture	$34,000	4.528	$153,952.00	
1975	William A. Goodman	Solirio	Sculpture	$12,000	4.528	$54,336.00	
1975	Silvia Heyden	Orientalisch	Textile	$1,650	4.528	$7,471.20	
1975	Silvia Heyden	Intervals	Textile	$1,500	4.528	$6,792.00	

	Artist	Title	Classification	Unadjusted Cost	Inflation Multiplier		Adjusted Annual Total
1976	Beverly Pepper	Excalibur	Sculpture	$98,000	4.281	$419,538.00	$4,472,360.70
1976	Lucas Samaras	Silent Struggle	Sculpture	$33,000	4.281	$141,273.00	
1976	Clement Meadmore	Out of There	Sculpture	$35,000	4.281	$149,835.00	
1976	Harold Balazs	Seattle Project	Sculpture	$11,000	4.281	$47,091.00	
1976	Bruce Beasley	Axial Incidence	Sculpture	$65,000	4.281	$278,265.00	
1976	Ilya Bolotowsky	Chicago Murals	Painting	$45,000	4.281	$192,645.00	
1976	Charles Ginnever	Protagoras	Sculpture	$42,500	4.281	$181,942.50	
1976	Lia Cook	Spatial Ikat III	Textile	$27,000	4.281	$115,587.00	
1976	Richard Hunt	Richmond Cycle	Sculpture	$70,000	4.281	$299,670.00	
1976	Annette Kaplan	Evolutionary Notes to WK	Textile	$7,000	4.281	$29,967.00	
1976	Lyman Kipp	Highline	Sculpture	$15,000	4.281	$64,215.00	
1976	Janet Kuemmerlein	Odyssey	Textile	$18,000	4.281	$77,058.00	
1976	Gyongy Laky	Inner Glyphs Out	Textile	$20,000	4.281	$85,620.00	
1976	Louise Nevelson	Bicentennial Dawn	Sculpture	$175,000	4.281	$749,175.00	
1976	Charles Ross	Origin of Color	Sculpture	$65,000	4.281	$278,265.00	
1976	Tony Smith	She Who Must Be Obeyed	Sculpture	$98,000	4.281	$419,538.00	
1976	Jack Youngerman	Rumi's Dance	Textile	$33,000	4.281	$141,273.00	
1976	Dimitri Hadzi	River Legend	Sculpture	$65,000	4.281	$278,265.00	
1976	John Paul Rietta	Force One Consciousness Is Crucial	Sculpture	$58,000	4.281	$248,298.00	
1976	George Segal	The Restaurant	Sculpture	$60,000	4.281	$256,860.00	
1976	Terry Weldon	Water Holes	Painting	$4,200	4.281	$17,980.20	

	Artist	Title	Classification	Unadjusted Cost	Inflation Multiplier		Adjusted Annual Total
1977	Mark di Suvero	Motu	Sculpture	$40,000	4.02	$160,800.00	$3,661,818.00
1977	Leonard Baskin	The Three Presidents from Tennessee	Sculpture	$30,000	4.02	$120,600.00	
1977	Marcel Breuer	Floating	Textile	$21,000	4.02	$84,420.00	
1977	Lin Emergy	Cane Dance	Sculpture	$13,500	4.02	$54,270.00	

	Artist	Title	Classification	Unadjusted Cost	Inflation Multiplier		Adjusted Annual Total
1977	Robert A. Howard	Louisville Project	Sculpture	$50,000	4.02	$201,000.00	
1977	Al Held	Order/Disorder/Ascension/Descension	Painting	$126,000	4.02	$506,520.00	
1977	Claes Oldenburg	Batcolumn	Sculpture	$100,000	4.02	$402,000.00	
1977	James Rosati	Heroic Shorepoints I	Sculpture	$64,000	4.02	$257,280.00	
1977	Charles Searles	Celebration	Painting	$30,000	4.02	$120,600.00	
1977	David Von Schlegell	Voyage of Ulysses	Sculpture	$175,000	4.02	$703,500.00	
1977	Peter Voulkos	Barking Sands	Sculpture	$40,000	4.02	$160,800.00	
1977	Jan Yoors	Symphony	Textile	$16,000	4.02	$64,320.00	
1977	Jack Beal	The History of Labor in America	Painting	$150,000	4.02	$603,000.00	
1977	Rudolph Heintz	Locations	Sculpture	$55,000	4.02	$221,100.00	
1977	Albert Edgar	North of Cunningham's	Photograph	$400	4.02	$1,608.00	
	Artist	**Title**	**Classification**	**Unadjusted Cost**	**Inflation Multiplier**		**Adjusted Annual Total**
1978	Stephen Antonakos	Red Neon Circle Fragments on a Blue Wall	Sculpture	$23,000	3.736	$85,928.00	$1,659,157.60
1978	Louise Bourgeois	Facets to the Sun	Sculpture	$35,000	3.736	$130,760.00	
1978	William King	Caring	Sculpture	$22,000	3.736	$82,192.00	
1978	Robert Mangold	Correlation: Two white line diagonals and two arcs with a 16 foot radius	Painting	$70,000	3.736	$261,520.00	
1978	John Geoffrey Naylor	Artifact	Sculpture	$30,000	3.736	$112,080.00	
1978	William Scott	Vigil	Sculpture	$10,000	3.736	$37,360.00	
1978	Blue Sky	Moonlight on the Great Pee Dee	Sculpture	$12,600	3.736	$47,073.60	
1978	Ned Smyth	Reverent Grove	Sculpture	$35,000	3.736	$130,760.00	
1978	George Sugarman	Baltimore Federal	Sculpture	$98,000	3.736	$366,128.00	
1978	James Surls	Sea Flower	Sculpture	$9,000	3.736	$33,624.00	
1978	Lenore Tawney	Cloud Series IV	Sculpture	$17,500	3.736	$65,380.00	
1978	Joseph Konzal	Gateway	Sculpture	$17,000	3.736	$63,512.00	
1978	George Rickey	Two Rectangles Excentric	Sculpture	$65,000	3.736	$242,840.00	
	Artist	**Title**	**Classification**	**Unadjusted Cost**	**Inflation Multiplier**		**Adjusted Annual Total**
1979	Alvin El Amason	Chignik Rose	Painting	$11,000	3.355	$36,905.00	$2,635,689.00
1979	James Wallace Buchman	Tablet	Sculpture	$9,500	3.355	$31,872.50	
1979	Jennifer Bartlett	Swimmers Atlanta	Painting	$110,000	3.355	$369,050.00	
1979	Guy Dill	Hoe Down	Sculpture	$25,600	3.355	$85,888.00	
1979	Sam Gilliam	Triple Varients	Painting	$50,000	3.355	$167,750.00	
1979	William Christenberry	Southern Wall	Sculpture	$30,000	3.355	$100,650.00	
1979	Gerald Conaway	Artic Amphibian	Sculpture	$21,000	3.355	$70,455.00	

Year	Artist	Title	Classification	Unadjusted Cost	Inflation Multiplier	Adjusted Annual Total	
1979	Lynne Golob Gellman	Pink 3/79	Painting	$3,500	3.355	$11,742.50	
1979	Lloyd Hamrol	Thronapolis	Sculpture	$45,000	3.355	$150,975.00	
1979	Rockne Krebs	The White Tornado	Sculpture	$50,000	3.355	$167,750.00	
1979	Sol LeWitt	One, Two, Three	Sculpture	$63,000	3.355	$211,365.00	
1979	Philip McCraken	Freedom	Sculpture	$11,000	3.355	$36,905.00	
1979	Robert Morris	untitled	Sculpture	$67,000	3.355	$224,785.00	
1979	Barbara Neijna	Right Turn on White	Sculpture	$65,000	3.355	$218,075.00	
1979	Roberto Rios	The Marla Section	Painting	$6,500	3.355	$21,807.50	
1979	Sylvia Stone	Dead Heat	Sculpture	$65,000	3.355	$218,075.00	
1979	Athena Tacha	Ripples	Sculpture	$50,000	3.355	$167,750.00	
1979	Marla Mallett	E Pluribus Unum	Sculpture	$25,000	3.355	$83,875.00	
1979	Ed McGowin	Mississippi Inscape	Sculpture	$50,000	3.355	$167,750.00	
1979	Douglas Moran	Southeast Wallscape Westgate	Painting	$8,500	3.355	$28,517.50	
1979	Rosemarie Castoro	Hexatryst	Sculpture	$19,000	3.355	$63,745.00	

Year	Artist	Title	Classification	Unadjusted Cost	Inflation Multiplier		Adjusted Annual Total
1980	Robert Arneson	Ikaros	Sculpture	$57,000	2.956	$168,492.00	$2,128,320.00
1980	Dale Chihuly	Pilchuk Baskets	Sculpture	$11,500	2.956	$33,994.00	
1980	Rafael Ferrer	Flotilla of Kayaks in a Tropical Storm	Sculpture	$45,000	2.956	$133,020.00	
1980	Dan Flavin	(untitled)	Sculpture	$80,000	2.956	$236,480.00	
1980	Richard Fleischner	Baltimore Project	Sculpture	$150,000	2.956	$443,400.00	
1980	Sam Francis	(untitled)	Painting	$98,000	2.956	$289,688.00	
1980	Robert Hudson	Tlingit	Sculpture	$90,000	2.956	$266,040.00	
1980	Alex Katz	(untitled)	Painting	$69,000	2.956	$203,964.00	
1980	George Morrison	Totem V	Sculpture	$10,000	2.956	$29,560.00	
1980	Roger Laux Nelson	First Day of Summer	Painting	$11,500	2.956	$33,994.00	
1980	Carmen Quinto Plunkett	The Thunderbirds	Sculpture	$4,000	2.956	$11,824.00	
1980	Carmen Quinto Plunkett	Tlingeit Conception II	Sculpture	$4,000	2.956	$11,824.00	
1980	Carmen Quinto Plunkett	The Protector	Sculpture	$4,000	2.956	$11,824.00	
1980	Murray Reich	Memphis Passage	Painting	$27,000	2.956	$79,812.00	
1980	Harris Shelton	Where to Look for Birds	Painting	$27,000	2.956	$79,812.00	
1980	Gaylen C. Hansen	Images of Palouse	Painting	$15,000	2.956	$44,340.00	
1980	Jackie Ferrera	Carbondale Project	Sculpture	$17,000	2.956	$50,252.00	

	Artist	Title	Classification	Unadjusted Cost	Inflation Multiplier		Adjusted Annual Total
1981	Ronald Bladen	Host of the Ellipse	Sculpture	$150,000	2.86	$429,000.00	$2,083,181.10
1981	Stan Dolega	(untitled)	Environmental Art	$19,000	2.86	$54,340.00	
1981	Stephen Henslin	Model Lady	Sculpture	$26,500	2.86	$75,790.00	
1981	Yvonne Jacquette	Autumn Expansion	Painting	$40,000	2.86	$114,400.00	
1981	Loren Madsen	Floating Ring	Sculpture	$125,000	2.86	$357,500.00	
1981	Kenneth Snelson	Tree I	Sculpture	$125,000	2.86	$357,500.00	
1981	Richard Serra	Tilted Arc	Sculpture	$175,000	2.86	$500,500.00	
1981	Isaac Witkin	Chorale	Sculpture	$15,000	2.86	$42,900.00	
1981	Herbert lee Creecy	Untitled	Painting	$1,200	2.86	$3,432.00	
1981	Kathleen E. Ferguson	Double Orange	Sculpture	$750	2.86	$2,145.00	
1981	Robert J. Franzini	Job IX	Print	$75	2.86	$214.50	
1981	Robert J. Franzini	Job VII	Print	$75	2.86	$214.50	
1981	Robert J. Franzini	Job VI	Print	$75	2.86	$214.50	
1981	Robert J. Franzini	Job II	Print	$75	2.86	$214.50	
1981	Robert J. Franzini	Job III	Print	$75	2.86	$214.50	
1981	Melody Guichet	The Gatekeeper I	Drawing	$250	2.86	$715.00	
1981	Melody Guichet	The Gatekeeper II	Drawing	$250	2.86	$715.00	
1981	Melody Guichet	Untitled	Painting	$400	2.86	$1,144.00	
1981	Donato Pietrodangelo	Parking Lot	Photograph	$125	2.86	$357.50	
1981	Donato Pietrodangelo	Metal Wall	Photograph	$130	2.86	$371.80	
1981	Donato Pietrodangelo	Pipe & Shadow	Photograph	$130	2.86	$371.80	
1981	Donato Pietrodangelo	Cardboard	Photograph	$130	2.86	$371.80	
1981	Donato Pietrodangelo	Yellow Pipes	Photograph	$140	2.86	$400.40	
1981	Donato Pietrodangelo	#1 and Shadow	Photograph	$140	2.86	$400.40	
1981	Edward Richard Pramuk	Veronica #5	Drawing	$150	2.86	$429.00	
1981	Edward Richard Pramuk	Veronica #6	Drawing	$150	2.86	$429.00	
1981	Edward Richard Pramuk	Veronica #10	Drawing	$150	2.86	$429.00	
1981	Edward Richard Pramuk	Veronica #13	Drawing	$150	2.86	$429.00	
1981	Edward Richard Pramuk	Veronica #14	Drawing	$150	2.86	$429.00	
1981	Jim Frazer	Rivers	Photograph	$200	2.86	$572.00	
1981	Jim Frazer	Photograph #2 - Sweetwater Falls, Douglas County	Photograph	$200	2.86	$572.00	

1981	Jim Frazer	Photograph #3 - Sweetwater Falls, Douglas County	Photograph	$200	2.86	$572.00	
1981	Jim Frazer	Photograph #4 - Sweetwater Falls, Douglas County	Photograph	$200	2.86	$572.00	
1981	Michael Smallwood	SUMO	Painting	$2,200	2.86	$6,292.00	
1981	Richard Lee Williams	Junction	Photograph	$300	2.86	$858.00	
1981	Richard Lee Williams	Store Front Modulation	Photograph	$300	2.86	$858.00	
1981	Richard Lee Williams	Shadow Space	Photograph	$300	2.86	$858.00	
1981	Richard Lee Williams	Carport	Photograph	$300	2.86	$858.00	
1981	Richard Lee Williams	Chinsegut Window	Photograph	$300	2.86	$858.00	
1981	Kathleen E. Ferguson	Flying Blue Electric	Sculpture	$700	2.86	$2,002.00	
1981	Kathleen E. Ferguson	Blue Electric with Pink	Sculpture	$750	2.86	$2,145.00	
1981	Carol Burch-Brown	Untitled #8	Drawing	$375	2.86	$1,072.50	
1981	Carol Burch-Brown	Untitled #6	Drawing	$375	2.86	$1,072.50	
1981	Carol Burch-Brown	Untitled #4	Drawing	$375	2.86	$1,072.50	
1981	Anna K. Burgess	Carnival	Textile	$650	2.86	$1,859.00	
1981	Curt Clyne	Cowboy in Coffee Shop	Photograph	$400	2.86	$1,144.00	
1981	Michael Anderson	Stellar Wheel	Sculpture	$1,000	2.86	$2,860.00	
1981	Sally Anderson	31 Flavors	Textile	$3,000	2.86	$8,580.00	
1981	Frederick J. Eversley	untitled	Sculpture	$4,200	2.86	$12,012.00	
1981	Betty Jo Kidson	Morning at Taos	Textile	$450	2.86	$1,287.00	
1981	Jane Knight	Double Layers	Textile	$700	2.86	$2,002.00	
1981	Dena Madole	Sun Form	Textile	$400	2.86	$1,144.00	
1981	Joyce Pardington	Canyon Wall #2	Textile	$400	2.86	$1,144.00	
1981	Joyce Pardington	October	Textile	$200	2.86	$572.00	
1981	Charles Pebworth	Lookout from San Bois	Sculpture	$6,500	2.86	$18,590.00	
1981	Rebecca Wheeler	Fur Piece	Textile	$800	2.86	$2,288.00	
1981	Charles Pratt	Night Riders	Sculpture	$700	2.86	$2,002.00	
1981	Terrie Mangat	Oklahoma Quilt	Textile	$1,500	2.86	$4,290.00	
1981	Bud Stainaker	Precise Notations	Textile	$750	2.86	$2,145.00	
1981	James Strickland	A Fallen Oak Tree	Sculpture	$2,100	2.86	$6,006.00	
1981	Melanie Vandenbos	Sunburst	Textile	$600	2.86	$1,716.00	
1981	Carol Whitney	Loyal Creek (A)	Sculpture	$250	2.86	$715.00	
1981	Carol Whitney	Loyal Creek (B)	Sculpture	$250	2.86	$715.00	
1981	W. A. Brown	Scanning Atlanta Streets	Photograph	$1,300	2.86	$3,718.00	

Appendix 107

Year	Artist	Title	Classification	Unadjusted Cost	Inflation Multiplier	Adjusted Annual Total
1981	Donato Pietrodangelo	Blue Sky and Orange Wall	Photograph	$140	2.86	$400.40	
1981	Jim Frazer	Photograph #5	Photograph	$200	2.86	$572.00
1981	Lisa Dru Irwin	Ladies Room	Photograph	$250	2.86	$715.00
1981	Lisa Dru Irwin	California Room	Photograph	$250	2.86	$715.00
1981	Lisa Dru Irwin	Arizona Café	Photograph	$250	2.86	$715.00
1981	Lisa Dru Irwin	Key West Window	Photograph	$250	2.86	$715.00
1981	Judy Voss Jones	This Is Beverly Silk	Print	$400	2.86	$1,144.00
1981	Judy Voss Jones	Larry's Egg	Print	$400	2.86	$1,144.00
1981	Judy Voss Jones	Willie Running After Wateau	Print	$400	2.86	$1,144.00
1981	Judy Voss Jones	Cat and Clock	Print	$300	2.86	$858.00
1981	Katherine Mitchell	Grid #1: Copper & Lavender	Print	$500	2.86	$1,430.00
1981	Katherine Mitchell	Drawing Thru a String-Grid: Silver & Gold	Print	$500	2.86	$1,430.00
1981	Katherine Mitchell	Gold/Silver Integration Series Drawing	Print	$500	2.86	$1,430.00
1981	Gayil Nalls	Formal Wear Ordeal	Painting	$950	2.86	$2,717.00
1981	Gayil Nalls	Façade Dada Ordeal	Painting	$950	2.86	$2,717.00
1981	Gayil Nalls	Near Washington Monument	Painting	$950	2.86	$2,717.00
1981	Richard Lee Williams	Contrail	Photograph	$300	2.86	$858.00
1981	Anna K. Burgess	Through the Looking Glass	Textile	$950	2.86	$2,717.00
1981	Karen Chapnick	Soaring Currents	Textile	$1,400	2.86	$4,004.00
1981	Curt Clyne	Winter Scene	Photograph	$400	2.86	$1,144.00
1981	Albert Edgar	Columbines at Cascade Canyon	Photograph	$400	2.86	$1,144.00
1981	David Halpern	Morning Mist	Photograph	$375	2.86	$1,072.50
1981	David Halpern	Charon's Sentinels	Photograph	$375	2.86	$1,072.50
1981	Jerry McMillan	Palm Tree Coil	Sculpture	$3,200	2.86	$9,152.00
1981	Frank Simons	Monolith	Sculpture	$300	2.86	$858.00
	Artist	**Title**	**Classification**	**Unadjusted Cost**	**Inflation Multiplier**	**Adjusted Annual Total**
1982	Lynda Benglis	Nalia	Sculpture	$35,000	2.524	$88,340.00	$514,896.00
1982	Lila Katzen	Floten Escort	Sculpture	$62,000	2.524	$156,488.00
1982	John Chamberlain	Detroit Deliquescence	Sculpture	$100,000	2.524	$252,400.00
1982	John Willenbecher	Untitled	Sculpture	$7,000	2.524	$17,668.00
	Artist	**Title**	**Classification**	**Unadjusted Cost**	**Inflation Multiplier**	**Adjusted Annual Total**
1983	Larry Bell	Moving Ways	Architectural arts	$55,000	2.446	$134,530.00	$341,461.60
1983	Robert Irwin	48 Shadow Planes	Sculpture	$84,600	2.446	$206,931.60

	Artist	Title	Classification	Unadjusted Cost	Inflation Multiplier		Adjusted Annual Total
1984	Robert Brooks	Clouds	Photograph	$4,000	2.345	$9,380.00	$268,502.50
1984	Ray King	Solar Wing	Architectural arts	$58,000	2.345	$136,010.00	
1984	Davjd Novros	Frescoes in Court-yard	Painting	$52,500	2.345	$123,112.50	
	Artist	Title	Classification	Unadjusted Cost	Inflation Multiplier		Adjusted Annual Total
1985	Terry Schoonhoven	(untitled)	Painting	$37,800	2.264	$85,579.20	$405,400.90
1985	Caleb Bach	The Effects of Good and Bad Government	Painting	$18,000	2.264	$40,752.00	
1985	Robert Longo	Sleep	Sculpture	$19,264	2.264	$43,613.70	
1985	George Nick	View of Boston over the Fort Point Channel	Painting	$29,000	2.264	$65,656.00	
1985	Patsy Norvell	Copper Heads	Sculpture	$25,000	2.264	$56,600.00	
1985	Edward Zucca	Untitled	Architectural arts	$50,000	2.264	$113,200.00	
	Artist	Title	Classification	Unadjusted Cost	Inflation Multiplier		Adjusted Annual Total
1986	Jane A. Kaufman	Crystal Hanging	Sculpture	$70,000	2.223	$155,610.00	$500,175.00
1986	Mary Miss	Cascading Wall Fountains	Architectural arts	$155,000	2.223	$344,565.00	
	Artist	Title	Classification	Unadjusted Cost	Inflation Multiplier		Adjusted Annual Total
1987	Maria Alquilar	Bien Venida Y Vaya Con Dios	Sculpture	$19,000	2.144	$40,736.00	$469,536.00
1987	Joel Schwartz	(untitled)	Architectural arts	$50,000	2.144	$107,200.00	
1987	Christopher Sproat	Untitled	Sculpture	$20,000	2.144	$42,880.00	
1987	Farley Tobin	(untitled)	Architectural arts	$30,000	2.144	$64,320.00	
1987	Robert Graham	San Jose Fountain	Architectural arts	$100,000	2.144	$214,400.00	
	Artist	Title	Classification	Unadjusted Cost	Inflation Multiplier		Adjusted Annual Total
1988	Melvin Edwards	Confirmation	Sculpture	$59,000	2.059	$121,481.00	$141,659.20
1988	Maxine Martell	Passage	Architectural arts	$9,800	2.059	$20,178.20	
	Artist	Title	Classification	Unadjusted Cost	Inflation Multiplier		Adjusted Annual Total
1989	Romare Bearden	Family	Architectural arts	$90,000	1.965	$176,850.00	$841,020.00
1989	Houston Conwill	Poets Rise	Sculpture	$49,000	1.965	$96,285.00	
1989	Jacob Lawrence	Community	Architectural arts	$95,000	1.965	$186,675.00	
1989	Manuel Neri	Ventana al Pacifico	Sculpture	$100,000	1.965	$196,500.00	
1989	Howardena Pindell	Queens Festival	Painting	$21,000	1.965	$41,265.00	
1989	Frank Smith	TRADITION: for Romare Bearden and Jacob Lawrence	Architectural arts	$20,000	1.965	$39,300.00	
1989	Edgar H. Sorrells-Adewale	Blessings	Sculpture	$20,000	1.965	$39,300.00	

Year	Artist	Title	Classification	Unadjusted Cost	Inflation Multiplier		Adjusted Annual Total
1989	Thomas A. Hardy	Savoy	Sculpture	$33,000	1.965	$64,845.00	
	Artist	**Title**	**Classification**	**Unadjusted Cost**	**Inflation Multiplier**		**Adjusted Annual Total**
1990	Jim Sanborn	Kryptos	Environmental art	$250,000	1.864	$466,000.00	$493,671.08
1990	Tad Savinar	Grass Is Greener	Architectural arts	$14,845	1.864	$27,671.08	
	Artist	**Title**	**Classification**	**Unadjusted Cost**	**Inflation Multiplier**		**Adjusted Annual Total**
1991	Scott Burton	Spillway Wall	Sculpture	$250,000	1.789	$447,250.00	$2,267,072.68
1991	Tom Otterness	The New World	Architectural arts	$266,000	1.789	$475,874.00	
1991	Joel Shapiro	(untitled)	Sculpture	$209,000	1.789	$373,901.00	
1991	A. Robert Bermelin	Paterson: The Aerialist, August 5, 1879	Painting	$36,000	1.789	$64,404.00	
1991	Richard Posner	Consumer's Lobby	Architectural arts	$39,000	1.789	$69,771.00	
1991	Jonathan Borofsky	Molecule Man 2 + 2	Sculpture	$295,000	1.789	$527,755.00	
1991	Luis A. Jimenez, Jr.	Fiesta Jarabe	Sculpture	$58,500	1.789	$104,656.50	
1991	Dimitri Hadzi	Red Mountain	Sculpture	$113,729	1.789	$203,461.18	
	Artist	**Title**	**Classification**	**Unadjusted Cost**	**Inflation Multiplier**		**Adjusted Annual Total**
1992	Ned Smyth	Two Worlds Apart	Sculpture	$115,000	1.736	$199,640.00	$483,476.00
1992	Kent Bloomer	(untitled)	Architectural arts	$20,500	1.736	$35,588.00	
1992	Timothy Woodman	Citizens	Sculpture	$33,000	1.736	$57,288.00	
1992	Stephen Robin	Cornucopiae	Sculpture	$110,000	1.736	$190,960.00	
	Artist	**Title**	**Classification**	**Unadjusted Cost**	**Inflation Multiplier**		**Adjusted Annual Total**
1993	Ed Carpenter	(untitled)	Architectural arts	$250,000	1.686	$421,500.00	$1,695,669.21
1993	Mary Lovelace O'Neal	Mermaid and Whales at Dinner	Painting	$12,500	1.686	$21,075.00	
1993	Mary Lovelace O'Neal	When Auntie Meets Mimi for Suchi	Painting	$12,500	1.686	$21,075.00	
1993	Nizette Brenan	Knoxville Flag	Sculpture	$75,000	1.686	$126,450.00	
1993	Jan Mitchell	Lady of Justice	Sculpture	$30,000	1.686	$50,580.00	
1993	Frank Stella	The Town-Ho's Story	Sculpture	$450,000	1.686	$758,700.00	
1993	John Valadez	A Day in El Paso del Norte	Painting	$50,300	1.686	$84,805.80	
1993	James D. Butler	Sunset Near the Chisholm Trail	Painting	$26,150	1.686	$44,088.90	
1993	James D. Butler	A View Near Tahlequah, Cherokee County	Painting	$26,150	1.686	$44,088.90	
1993	Jaime Suarez	Totemic Sculpture	Sculpture	$40,000	1.686	$67,440.00	
1993	Leo Carty	The Legacy of the Virgin Islands	Painting	$14,135	1.686	$23,831.61	
1993	Malou Flato	South Texas Palm Trees	Painting	$19,000	1.686	$32,034.00	

	Artist	Title	Classification	Unadjusted Cost	Inflation Multiplier		Adjusted Annual Total
1994	Oliver L. Jackson	(untitled)	Sculpture	$114,500	1.644	$188,238.00	$1,641,127.93
1994	Diana Moore	Justice	Sculpture	$125,000	1.644	$205,500.00	
1994	Albert Paley	Metamorphosis	Architectural arts	$129,000	1.644	$212,076.00	
1994	Richard Haas	Justice and the Prairie	Painting	$172,775	1.644	$284,042.10	
1994	Joseph Di Stefano	Your Memory Column	Sculpture	$89,500	1.644	$147,138.00	
1994	Arthur Stern	Torchere	Architectural arts	$26,146	1.644	$42,984.02	
1994	Arthur Stern	Sentinels	Architectural arts	$26,146	1.644	$42,984.02	
1994	Arthur Stern	Tall Sentinels	Architectural arts	$26,146	1.644	$42,984.02	
1994	Roger Laux Nelson	High Plains	Painting	$15,000	1.644	$24,660.00	
1994	Roger Laux Nelson	Prairie	Painting	$15,000	1.644	$24,660.00	
1994	Mark Strand	(untitled poem)	Poetry	$2,000	1.644	$3,288.00	
1994	Malou Flato	Fort Brown Resaca	Painting	$20,000	1.644	$32,880.00	
1994	John Valadez	The Coming of Rain	Painting	$52,040	1.644	$85,553.76	
1994	Clyde Lynds	Passage	Sculpture	$57,000	1.644	$93,708.00	
1994	Daniel Sprick	Federal Courthouse Diptych #1	Painting	$22,500	1.644	$36,990.00	
1994	Daniel Sprick	Federal Courthouse Diptych #2	Painting	$22,500	1.644	$36,990.00	
1994	Merrill Mahaffey	Lodore Canyon	Painting	$25,000	1.644	$41,100.00	
1994	Joellyn T. Duesberry	April in Colorado	Painting	$12,500	1.644	$20,550.00	
1994	Joellyn T. Duesberry	April in New Mexico	Painting	$12,500	1.644	$20,550.00	
1994	Jon Eric Riis	Grey Patina	Textile	$2,500	1.644	$4,110.00	
1994	Gary Trentham	Glad Wrap Form	Sculpture	$3,000	1.644	$4,932.00	
1994	Street Singing, 1993-1994	Raymond Saunders	Sculpture	$27,500	1.644	$45,210.00	
	Artist	Title	Classification	Unadjusted Cost	Inflation Multiplier		Adjusted Annual Total
1995	Judith Brown	(untitled)	Sculpture	$129,695	1.598	$207,252.61	$3,316,316.62
1995	Jenny Holzer	Allentown Benches: Selections from Truisms & Survival Stories	Architectural arts	$70,000	1.598	$111,860.00	
1995	Linda Howard	Sky Cathedral	Sculpture	$40,000.00	1.598	$63,920.00	
1995	Albert Paley	Passage	Sculpture	$147,535	1.598	$235,760.93	
1995	Jill Sablosky	A Course in Change	Sculpture	$21,000	1.598	$33,558.00	
1995	Michael A. Naranjo	Justice	Sculpture	$18,672	1.598	$29,837.86	
1995	Raymond Kaskey	Justice Delayed, Justice Denied	Sculpture	$283,000	1.598	$452,234.00	
1995	Clyde Lynds	America Song	Sculpture	$350,000	1.598	$559,300.00	

1995	Jim Sanborn	Indian Run	Environmental art	$170,000	1.598	$271,660.00	
1995	Barbara Grygutis	Portal	Sculpture	$61,500	1.598	$98,277.00	
1995	Michael Hachey	A Wall for Quock Walker	Painting	$60,000	1.598	$95,880.00	
1995	Raymond Kaskey	Justice and the Sundial	Sculpture	$108,890	1.598	$174,006.22	
1995	Houston Conwill	The New Ring Shout	Architectural arts	$450,000	1.598	$719,100.00	
1995	Roger Brown	(untitled)	Architectural arts	$100,000	1.598	$159,800.00	
1995	Bob Haozous	Spirit of the Earth	Sculpture	$65,000	1.598	$103,870.00	

	Artist	Title	Classification	Unadjusted Cost	Inflation Multiplier		Adjusted Annual Total
1996	Rachel Hecker	Fill Every Pause along the Way	Painting	$15,000	1.553	$23,295.00	$2,286,016.00
1996	Maya Lin	Sounding Stones	Sculpture	$400,000	1.553	$621,200.00	
1996	Gail Niebrugge	The Prospector's Trail	Painting	$38,000	1.553	$59,014.00	
1996	Mark Allen Lere	Seven Sculptures	Environmental art	$165,000	1.553	$256,245	
1996	Marrilynn Adams	Tulsey Judicial Window	Architectural arts	$40,000	1.553	$62,120	
1996	Michael Helzer	Perforated Object	Sculpture	$82,500	1.553	$128,122.50	
1996	Michael Helzer	Perforation	Sculpture	$82,500	1.553	$128,122.50	
1996	Douglas Hollis	Watersongs	Architectural arts	$185,000	1.553	$287,305.00	
1996	Robert Lobe	Harmony Ridge	Sculpture	$34,000	1.553	$52,802.00	
1996	Beverly Pepper	Manhattan Sentinels	Sculpture	$377,000	1.553	$585,481.00	
1996	Dorothea Rockburne	The Virtues of Good Government	Painting	$53,000	1.553	$82,309.00	

	Artist	Title	Classification	Unadjusted Cost	Inflation Multiplier		Adjusted Annual Total
1997	Milton Glaser	Color Fuses	Painting	$50,000	1.518	$75,900.00	$6,995,488.96
1997	Jim Sanborn	Ex Nexum	Sculpture	$61,859	1.518	$93,901.96	
1997	Martin Puryear	Bearing Witness	Sculpture	$1,000,000	1.518	$1,518,000.00	
1997	Keith Sonnier	Route Zenith	Architectural arts	$700,000	1.518	$1,062,600.00	
1997	Stephen Robin	Federal Triangle Flowers	Sculpture	$300,000	1.518	$455,400.00	
1997	Judith Poxson Fawkes	Justice	Textile	$25,000	1.518	$37,950.00	
1997	Judith Poxson Fawkes	Oregon	Textile	$25,000	1.518	$37,950.00	
1997	Judith Poxson Fawkes	Judicial Heritage	Textile	$25,000	1.518	$37,950.00	
1997	Judith Poxson Fawkes	Oregeon Environment	Textile	$25,000	1.518	$37,950.00	
1997	John R. Briggs	Turtle Key	Painting	$41,250	1.518	$62,617.50	
1997	John R. Briggs	Peace River	Painting	$41,250	1.518	$62,617.50	
1997	John R. Briggs	Big Cypress	Painting	$41,250	1.518	$62,617.50	

Year	Artist	Title	Classification	Unadjusted Cost	Inflation Multiplier	Adjusted Annual Total	
1997	John R. Briggs	Sabal Palm, State Tree	Painting	$41,250	1.518	$62,617.50	
1997	Ahearn and Torres	Life in the Community - East 100th Street	Sculpture	$155,000	1.518	$235,290.00	
1997	Ahearn and Torres	Homage to Medicare and Medicaid	Sculpture	$155,000	1.518	$235,290.00	
1997	Roberto L. Delgado	La Raza Ambulante - The People Walking	Architectural arts	$26,000	1.518	$39,468.00	
1997	Susan T. Gamble	The Naco Borderland	Architectural arts	$16,000	1.518	$24,288.00	
1997	Katherine Pond	SUNFIX for Judy	Sculpture	$32,000	1.518	$48,576.00	
1997	Diana Moore	Justice	Sculpture	$170,000	1.518	$258,060.00	
1997	Keith Sonnier	Cenozoic Codex	Architectural arts	$145,000	1.518	$220,110.00	
1997	Larry Kirkland	Vox Populi	Sculpture	$400,000	1.518	$607,200.00	
1997	Frederick J. Eversley	(untitled)	Sculpture	$150,000	1.518	$227,700.00	
1997	Eric Orr	Ocean of Thought	Sculpture	$150,000	1.518	$227,700.00	
1997	Eric Orr	Passage of Time	Sculpture	$150,000	1.518	$227,700.00	
1997	Eric Orr	Portland Water Veil	Sculpture	$150,000	1.518	$227,700.00	
1997	Tom Otterness	Law of Nature	Sculpture	$500,000	1.518	$759,000.00	
1997	Sandra Stone	(untitled)	Poetry	$15,000	1.518	$22,770.00	
1997	Arthur Stern	Torchere	Sculpture	$17,500	1.518	$26,565.00	
	Artist	**Title**	**Classification**	**Unadjusted Cost**	**Inflation Multiplier**	**Adjusted Annual Total**	
1998	Alexander Liberman	On High	Sculpture	$100,000	1.494	$149,400.00	$6,096,189.31
1998	Raymond Kaskey	Boundary Markers	Sculpture	$167,000	1.494	$249,498.00	
1998	Beverly Pepper	The Sentinels of Justice	Sculpture	$450,000	1.494	$672,300.00	
1998	Barbara Cloud-Riboud	Africa Rising	Sculpture	$220,000	1.494	$328,680.00	
1998	Tomie Arai	Renewal	Painting	$80,000	1.494	$119,520.00	
1998	Ellsworth Kelly	The Boston Panels	Sculpture	$800,000	1.494	$1,195,200.00	
1998	David Wilson	(untitled)	Architectural arts	$300,000	1.494	$448,200.00	
1998	Sam Gilliam	Color of Medals	Painting	$250,000	1.494	$373,500.00	
1998	Daniel Galvez	For the Love of Life	Painting	$50,000	1.494	$74,700.00	
1998	Daniel Galvez	The Healing Light	Painting	$50,000	1.494	$74,700.00	
1998	Susan Furini	Sasabe	Sculpture	$15,000	1.494	$22,410.00	
1998	Charles Ross	Solar Spectrum	Sculpture	$250,000	1.494	$373,500.00	
1998	Vicki Scuri	Eagle Template	Architectural arts	$70,000	1.494	$104,580.00	
1998	John Valadez	We the People: Summer Festivals in Orange County	Painting	$320,000	1.494	$478,080.00	
1998	Raymond Kaskey	Power of the Law	Sculpture	$131,500	1.494	$196,461.00	
1998	Raymond Kaskey	Wisdom of the Law	Sculpture	$131,500	1.494	$196,461.00	

Year	Artist	Title	Classification	Unadjusted Cost	Inflation Multiplier		Adjusted Annual Total
1998	Sally Apfelbaum	Conservatory Pond	Photograph	$13,500	1.494	$20,169.00	
1998	Sally Apfelbaum	Angel of the Waters	Photograph	$13,500	1.494	$20,169.00	
1998	Alison Sky	Milagros Imigrando/ Migrating Miracles	Sculpture	$75,448	1.494	$112,719.31	
1998	Steven Woodward	Monument to Monument	Sculpture	$48,000	1.494	$71,712.00	
1998	Clyde Lynds	Sentinel	Sculpture	$250,000	1.494	$373,500.00	
1998	Jeff G. Smith	Art Glass	Architectural arts	$75,000	1.494	$112,050.00	
1998	Michael Singer	Healing Garden	Architectural arts	$220,000	1.494	$328,680.00	
	Artist	**Title**	**Classification**	**Unadjusted Cost**	**Inflation Multiplier**		**Adjusted Annual Total**
1999	Rebecca Bluestone	Four Corners Triptych	Textile	$36,000	1.462	$52,632.00	$4,218,203.34
1999	Tom Otterness	Rockman	Sculpture	$396,500	1.462	$579,683.00	
1999	Tom Otterness	Gold Rush	Sculpture	$250,000	1.462	$365,500.00	
1999	Larry Kirkland	The Decisions	Sculpture	$175,000	1.462	$255,850.00	
1999	C. G. Simonds	Beam Ends	Sculpture	$21,000	1.462	$30,702.00	
1999	Jenny Holzer	Installation for the U.S. Courthouse and Federal Building	Architectural arts	$75,000	1.462	$109,650.00	
1999	Rita Dove	(untitled)	Architectural arts	$13,000	1.462	$19,006.00	
1999	Deborah Oropallo	China Pattern	Painting	$20,000	1.462	$29,240.00	
1999	Diana Moore	Urns of Justice	Sculpture	$125,000	1.462	$182,750.00	
1999	Barbara Jo Revelle	The Alternative History of Fort Myers	Photograph	$188,500	1.462	$275,587.00	
1999	Lincoln Perry	One Nation, Under Law	Painting	$105,000	1.462	$153,510.00	
1999	Caroline Court	Penelopeia	Sculpture	$43,000	1.462	$62,866.00	
1999	Jim Sanborn	Binary Systems	Sculpture	$215,000	1.462	$314,330.00	
1999	Tony Berlant	On This Spot Stood the First Chinese Settlement in Sacramento	Sculpture	$15,000	1.462	$21,930.00	
1999	Daniel Galvez	Golden Mountains/ Golden Fields	Painting	$15,000	1.462	$21,930.00	
1999	Steve Gillman	Passage No. 3	Sculpture	$21,000	1.462	$30,702.00	
1999	Holley Junker	Chinadom	Textile	$3,000	1.462	$4,386.00	
1999	Kathleen Kasper-Noonan	World Lines: Mapping the Journey of the Spirit and Reason, In Memory of My Father	Sculpture	$10,000	1.462	$14,620.00	
1999	George Miyasaki	Dream within a Dream: In Honor of the Pacific Asian Pioneers	Painting	$12,000	1.462	$17,544.00	
1999	Jack Nielsen	The Agreement	Sculpture	$21,000	1.462	$30,702.00	
1999	Clyde Lynds	Martinsburg, Red, White, & Blue	Sculpture	$100,000	1.462	$146,200.00	

	Artist	Title	Classification	Unadjusted Cost	Inflation Multiplier		Adjusted Annual Total
1999	Susan Poffenbarger	South Branch Bend	Painting	$5,000	1.462	$7,310.00	
1999	Paul Housberg	Lightfall	Architectural arts	$120,000	1.462	$175,440.00	
1999	Enzo Torcoletti	Concurrence Gateway	Sculpture	$134,099	1.462	$196,052.74	
1999	Kenneth F. vonRoenn Jr.	(untitled)	Architectural arts	$84,000	1.462	$122,808.00	
1999	Richard Haas	Justice in West Virginia	Painting	$138,000	1.462	$201,756.00	
1999	Stephen Robin	Nebraska Grilles	Architectural arts	$250,000	1.462	$365,500.00	
1999	Bennett Brien	Millenium	Sculpture	$34,500	1.462	$50,439.00	
1999	Laurence Holden	The Four Seasons	Painting	$80,629	1.462	$117,879.60	
1999	Doug Hyde	(untitled)	Sculpture	$179,000	1.462	$261,698.00	
	Artist	**Title**	**Classification**	**Unadjusted Cost**	**Inflation Multiplier**		**Adjusted Annual Total**
2000	Audrey Flack	Beloved Women of Justice	Sculpture	$65,000	1.415	$91,975.00	$2,602,735.44
2000	Helmick and Schecter	Jurisprudents	Sculpture	$42,522	1.415	$60,168.63	
2000	Lita Albuquerque	Gardens of Remembrance	Architectural arts	$242,500	1.415	$343,137.50	
2000	Jim Wald	Sonoran Spring	Painting	$75,000	1.415	$106,125.00	
2000	Clyde Lynds	Objective	Architectural arts	$200,117	1.415	$283,165.56	
2000	James Carpenter	Lens Ceiling	Architectural arts	$800,000	1.415	$1,132,000.00	
2000	Howard Ben Tre	Vortex, Stream, and Confluence	Architectural arts	$330,000	1.415	$466,950.00	
2000	Connie Lloveras	Peace Threshold	Painting	$22,500	1.415	$31,837.50	
2000	Willard Dixon	Red Rock Canyon	Painting	$50,000	1.415	$70,750.00	
2000	Brent Thomson	Eldorado	Painting	$11,750	1.415	$16,626.25	
	Artist	**Title**	**Classification**	**Unadjusted Cost**	**Inflation Multiplier**		**Adjusted Annual Total**
2001	Winifred Lutz	Zones of Change	Environmental art	$200,000	1.376	$275,200.00	$560,720.00
2001	Michele Oka Doner	Poplar and Iris	Sculpture	$112,500	1.376	$154,800.00	
2001	Michaela Mahady	La Frontera	Architectural arts	$95,000	1.376	$130,720.00	
	Artist	**Title**	**Classification**	**Unadjusted Cost**	**Inflation Multiplier**		**Adjusted Annual Total**
2002	Pat Benincasa	Moon Boat & Night Sky Glass	Sculpture	$38,000	1.354	$51,452.00	$1,293,510.05
2002	Andrew Leicester	Phantom Furnace Columns	Sculpture	$60,000	1.354	$81,240.00	
2002	Valerie Jaudon	Portal North	Painting	$100,000	1.354	$135,400.00	
2002	Valerie Jaudon	Portal South	Painting	$100,000	1.354	$135,400.00	
2002	Tom Askman	Wings	Sculpture	$47,900	1.354	$64,856.60	
2002	Peter Shire	Imaginary Line, Concrete Connection	Sculpture	$70,000	1.354	$94,780.00	
2002	Arturo Alonzo Sandoval	Appalachian Knobs	Sculpture	$16,250	1.354	$22,002.50	

Year	Artist	Title	Classification	Unadjusted Cost	Inflation Multiplier	Adjusted Annual Total	
2002	Arturo Alonzo Sandoval	Appalachian Thaw	Sculpture	$16,250	1.354	$22,002.50	
2002	Arturo Alonzo Sandoval	Appalachian Laurel	Sculpture	$16,250	1.354	$22,002.50	
2002	Arturo Alonzo Sandoval	Appalachian Autumn	Sculpture	$16,250	1.354	$22,002.50	
2002	Dale Chihuly	Hammond Courthouse Installation	Sculpture	$194,000	1.354	$262,676.00	
2002	Raymond Kaskey	Jury Duty	Sculpture	$104,925	1.354	$142,068.45	
2002	Maria Artemis	Epigenesis	Environmental art	$112,500	1.354	$152,325.00	
2002	Richard Davis	Storm	Sculpture	$7,000	1.354	$9,478.00	
2002	Grant Speed	Riders in the Distances Add to the Risks of Rustlin'	Sculpture	$6,000	1.354	$8,124.00	
2002	Hung Liu	Nightingale	Painting	$25,000	1.354	$33,850.00	
2002	Rupert Garcia	1965, 1970, 2002, 2002	Painting	$25,000	1.354	$33,850.00	
	Artist	**Title**	**Classification**	**Unadjusted Cost**	**Inflation Multiplier**		**Adjusted Annual Total**
2003	Michele Oka Doner	Wave and Gate	Architectural arts	$159,000	1.324	$210,516.00	$1,657,648.00
2003	Molly Mabe	The Ancient Palms Within	Painting	$20,000	1.324	$26,480.00	
2003	Sol LeWitt	Irregular Form	Architectural arts	$100,000	1.324	$132,400.00	
2003	Susan Kaprov	Swimmers	Architectural arts	$130,000	1.324	$172,120.00	
2003	Jim Dire	Cleveland Venus	Sculpture	$708,000	1.324	$937,392.00	
2003	Michele Oka Doner	River of Quintessence	Architectural arts	$110,000	1.324	$145,640.00	
2003	William T. Wiley	Will We Get Here Now	Painting	$25,000	1.324	$33,100.00	
	Artist	**Title**	**Classification**	**Unadjusted Cost**	**Inflation Multiplier**		**Adjusted Annual Total**
2004	Mikyoung Kim	River of Light	Sculpture	$70,000	1.29	$90,300.00	$3,220,523.70
2004	Tracy Linder	Forces of Labor	Sculpture	$26,035	1.29	$33,585.15	
2004	Susan Poffenbarger	View from Suspension Bridge	Painting	$5,000	1.29	$6,450.00	
2004	Patricia Leighton & Del Geist	Passage	Environmental art	$34,460	1.29	$44,453.40	
2004	David Wilson	(untitled)	Architectural arts	$50,000	1.29	$64,500.00	
2004	Philip Simmons	(untitled)	Architectural arts	$145,000	1.29	$187,050.00	
2004	Brad J. Goldberg	Foundation	Environmental art	$75,000	1.29	$96,750.00	
2004	Douglas Hollis	Star Field	Architectural arts	$75,000	1.29	$96,750.00	
2004	Alice Aycock	Swing Over	Sculpture	$350,000	1.29	$451,500.00	
2004	Ed Carpenter	Leaf	Sculpture	$450,000	1.29	$580,500.00	
2004	Ming Fay	Pillar Arc	Sculpture	$300,000	1.29	$387,000.00	

	Artist	Title	Classification	Unadjusted Cost	Inflation Multiplier		Adjusted Annual Total
2004	Paul Marioni, Ann Troutner	Reflection Fountain	Architectural arts	$125,000	1.29	$161,250.00	
2004	Michael Fajans	Three Sets of Twelves	Painting	$90,000	1.29	$116,100.00	
2004	Sung-Ho Choi	Quiltroad	Painting	$35,000	1.29	$45,150.00	
2004	Deborah Mersky	Winding Ribbon	Architectural arts	$45,000	1.29	$58,050.00	
2004	Deborah Mersky	Forest Gates	Architectural arts	$45,000	1.29	$58,050.00	
2004	Valerie Jaudon	Filippine Garden	Environmental art	$550,000	1.29	$709,500.00	
2004	Tracy Linder	Backbone	Sculpture	$26,035	1.29	$33,585.15	
	Artist	**Title**	**Classification**	**Unadjusted Cost**	**Inflation Multiplier**		**Adjusted Annual Total**
2005	Frank Stella	Hooloomooloo IV, 1994–2005	Painting	$875,000	1.247	$1,091,125.00	$2,393,024.18
2005	Terrence Karpowicz	Independence Crossing	Architectural arts	$60,000	1.247	$74,820.00	
2005	Masayuki Oda	Land Art Project, Tecate, Calif. 2005	Sculpture	$44,125	1.247	$55,023.88	
2005	Maya Lin	Flutter	Environmental art	$150,000	1.247	$187,050.00	
2005	Murch and Hollis	Once Upon a Time in Fresno	Architectural arts	$400,000	1.247	$498,800.00	
2005	Adam Longatti	The Height of Spring	Painting	$5,000	1.247	$6,235.00	
2005	Adam Longatti	The End of Summer	Painting	$5,000	1.247	$6,235.00	
2005	Brian Shure	Gateway Center from Ninth Street Bridge	Painting	$23,300	1.247	$29,055.10	
2005	Brian Shure	Fourth and Market, PRG Center	Painting	$23,300	1.247	$29,055.10	
2005	Brian Shure	South Side, East Carson and Twelfth	Painting	$23,300	1.247	$29,055.10	
2005	Mark Calderon	Concordia	Sculpture	$35,000	1.247	$43,645.00	
2005	Lisa Scheer	Beacon	Sculpture	$275,000	1.247	$342,925.00	
	Artist	**Title**	**Classification**	**Unadjusted Cost**	**Inflation Multiplier**		**Adjusted Annual Total**
2006	Jim Campbell	Broken Wall	Time-based media	$195,000	1.208	$235,560.00	$2,691,992.97
2006	Jim Campbell	The Colorado	Time-based media	$195,000	1.208	$235,560.00	
2006	Al Held	(untitled)	Architectural arts	$378,210	1.208	$456,877.68	
2006	Matthew Ritchie	Stare Decisis	Sculpture	$406,119	1.208	$490,591.75	
2006	Matthew Ritchie	Life	Print	$100,000	1.208	$120,800.00	
2006	Matthew Ritchie	Liberty	Print	$100,000	1.208	$120,800.00	
2006	Matthew Ritchie	Pursuit	Print	$100,000	1.208	$120,800.00	
2006	Arturo Herrera	Night Before Last/ Chicago	Painting	$100,000	1.208	$120,800.00	
2006	Xiaoze Xie	The Spirit of the Law	Painting	$25,000	1.208	$30,200.00	
2006	Xiaoze Xie	Iowa Reports	Painting	$25,000	1.208	$30,200.00	
2006	Cris Bruch	Shortest Distance	Sculpture	$139,252	1.208	$168,216.42	

Year	Artist	Title	Classification	Unadjusted Cost	Inflation Multiplier		Adjusted Annual Total
2006	Sean Healy	Jury Pool	Architectural arts	$50,000	1.208	$60,400.00	
2006	Kristen Timken	Witness	Photograph	$75,000	1.208	$90,600.00	
2006	Lia Cook	Sons and Daughters	Textile	$180,000	1.208	$217,440.00	
2006	Inigo Manglano-Ovalle	La Tormenta/The Storm	Sculpture	$159,890	1.208	$193,147.12	
Year	**Artist**	**Title**	**Classification**	**Unadjusted Cost**	**Inflation Multiplier**		**Adjusted Annual Total**
2007	Edward Ruscha	Maps, DNA and Spam	Architectural arts	$37,500	1.175	$44,062.50	$1,726,799.98
2007	Edward Ruscha	Don't Nod	Architectural arts	$37,500	1.175	$44,062.50	
2007	Edward Ruscha	I Did Did I?	Architectural arts	$37,500	1.175	$44,062.50	
2007	Edward Ruscha	Level as Level	Architectural arts	$37,500	1.175	$44,062.50	
2007	James Turrell	Skygarden	Architectural arts	$250,000	1.175	$293,750.00	
2007	Clyde Butcher	Florida Trail	Photograph	$2,885	1.175	$3,389.88	
2007	Clyde Butcher	Estero Island	Photograph	$5,150	1.175	$6,051.25	
2007	Clyde Butcher	Three Sisters	Photograph	$2,885	1.175	$3,389.88	
2007	Ned Kahn	Quantum Wave	Sculpture	$395,000	1.175	$464,125.00	
2007	Sam Gilliam	Census in Suitland	Painting	$100,000	1.175	$117,500.00	
2007	Nathan Farb	Little Cherrypatch Pond	Photograph	$30,000	1.175	$35,250.00	
2007	Nathan Farb	Weller Pond Outlet	Photograph	$30,000	1.175	$35,250.00	
2007	Anita Glesta	Census Walk of Numbers	Environmental art	$408,697	1.175	$480,218.98	
2007	Tim Rollins and K.O.S.	EVERYONE IS WELCOME! For the People of Fargo (after Franz Kafka)	Painting	$95,000	1.175	$111,625.00	
Year	**Artist**	**Title**	**Classification**	**Unadjusted Cost**	**Inflation Multiplier**		**Adjusted Annual Total**
2008	Pae White	Bug Screen	Sculpture	$269,000	1.131	$304,239.00	$1,159,481.97
2008	Sol Lewitt	Wall Drawing #1259/ Loopy Doopy (Springfield)	Painting	$133,000	1.131	$150,423.00	
2008	Mikyoung Kim	Echo Dynamics	Environmental	$284,183	1.131	$321,410.97	
2008	Jean Shin	Dress Code	Textile	$150,000	1.131	$169,650.00	
2008	Patrick Zentz	Wind Chimes	Time-based media	$54,000	1.131	$61,074.00	
2008	Ann Brauer	Hills, Fields, River and Two Trees: Scenes from Western Massachusetts	Textile	$75,000	1.131	$84,825.00	
2008	Stephen Batura	Tucson Trio	Painting	$20,000	1.131	$22,620.00	
2008	James Cook	Pima Canyon	Painting	$20,000	1.131	$22,620.00	
2008	Howard Post	Behind a Mountain	Painting	$20,000	1.131	$22,620.00	

	Artist	Title	Classification	Unadjusted Cost	Inflation Multiplier		Adjusted Annual Total
2009	Aaron T. Stephan	Intersect	Sculpture	$114,500	1.135	$129,957.50	$1,199,848.23
2009	Nade Haley	Windhorse	Photograph	$55,000	1.135	$62,425.00	
2009	Sean Healy	Gesture Politics	Architectural arts	$200,000	1.135	$227,000.00	
2009	Jason Salavon	American Varietal	Sculpture	$462,635	1.135	$525,090.73	
2009	Alan Michelson	Third Bank of the River	Architectural arts	$225,000	1.135	$255,375.00	
	Artist	Title	Classification	Unadjusted Cost	Inflation Multiplier		Adjusted Annual Total
2010	Allan McCollum	FDA Shapes Project	Sculpture	$356,000	1.117	$397,652.00	$2,048,755.60
2010	Fletcher Cox	(untitled - courtroom doors)	Architectural arts	$95,159	1.117	$106,292.60	
2010	Jose Galvez	Patriotismo/ Patriotism	Photograph	$30,000	1.117	$33,510.00	
2010	Miguel Gandert	Alma del Pueblo/ Soul of the People	Photograph	$30,000	1.117	$33,510.00	
2010	David Taylor	Frontier/Frontera (Version 2)	Photograph	$15,000	1.117	$16,755.00	
2010	David Taylor	Fenceline, Tecate Peak, U.S.-Mexico Border	Photograph	$15,000	1.117	$16,755.00	
2010	Lead Pencil Studios	Non-Sign II	Sculpture	$200,000	1.117	$223,400.00	
2010	Helen Mirra	Roseau County Bird Rainbow	Drawing	$28,000	1.117	$31,276.00	
2010	Helen Mirra	TamarackColor Index	Environmental art	$150,000	1.117	$167,550.00	
2010	Larry Kirkland	Obelisk	Sculpture	$100,000	1.117	$111,700.00	
2010	Larry Kirkland	Portal	Sculpture	$100,000	1.117	$111,700.00	
2010	Dan McCleary	American Jury	Painting	$200,000	1.117	$223,400.00	
2010	Leo Villareal	Sky	Time-based media	$200,000	1.117	$223,400.00	
2010	Jeff Schmuki	Pearl River	Sculpture	$35,000	1.117	$39,095.00	
2010	Anna Valentina Murch	Reflections on a Landscape	Textile	$100,000	1.117	$111,700.00	
2010	Inigo Manglano-Ovalle	Redberg	Sculpture	$180,000	1.117	$201,060.00	
	Artist	Title	Classification	Unadjusted Cost	Inflation Multiplier		Adjusted Annual Total
2011	Roberto Juarez	Fort Pierce Courthouse Murals (Cultural Law/Natural Justice)	Painting	$130,000	1.083	$140,790.00	$1,602,840.00
2011	Tony Feher	Super Special Happy Place	Environmental art	$250,000	1.083	$270,750.00	
2011	Do Ho Suh	Screen at FDA	Sculpture	$350,000	1.083	$379,050.00	
2011	Robert Mangold	Three Columns	Architectural arts	$400,000	1.083	$433,200.00	
2011	Katy Stone	(cloudwaterline) Horizon	Sculpture	$350,000	1.083	$379,050.00	

	Artist	Title	Classification	Unadjusted Cost	Inflation Multiplier		Adjusted Annual Total
2012	Jenny Holzer	For the FDA	Architectural arts	$700,000	1.061	$742,700.00	$3,534,406.38
2012	Clifford Ross	The Austin Wall	Architectural arts	$424,035	1.061	$449,901.14	
2012	Robert Irwin	Hedge Wedge	Environmental art	$535,000	1.061	$567,635.00	
2012	Caleb O'Connor	Points in Time: The Tuscaloosa Murals	Painting	$201,792	1.061	$214,101.31	
2012	Fred Easker	Iowa August	Painting	$15,000	1.061	$15,915.00	
2012	Lucinda Parker	Deliverance of Water	Painting	$29,600	1.061	$31,405.60	
2012	Lucinda Parker	Aqueduct	Painting	$29,600	1.061	$31,405.60	
2012	Lucinda Parker	Head Waters	Painting	$29,600	1.061	$31,405.60	
2012	Lucinda Parker	Elixir in a Dry Land	Painting	$29,600	1.061	$31,405.60	
2012	Lucinda Parker	Canyon Song	Painting	$29,600	1.061	$31,405.60	
2012	Ellen Harvey	Fossils	Sculpture	$225,000	1.061	$238,725.00	
2012	Ellen Wagener	Iowa Summer	Drawing	$10,000	1.061	$10,610.00	
2012	Ellen Wagener	Iowa Autumn	Drawing	$10,000	1.061	$10,610.00	
2012	Ellen Wagener	Iowa Winter	Drawing	$10,000	1.061	$10,610.00	
2012	Ellen Wagener	Iowa Spring	Drawing	$10,000	1.061	$10,610.00	
2012	Betty Woodman	River View	Painting	$287,376	1.061	$304,905.94	
2012	Buster Simpson	Aerie	Sculpture	$305,000	1.061	$323,605.00	
2012	Ralph Helmick	E Pluribus	Sculpture	$450,000	1.061	$477,450.00	
	Artist	Title	Classification	Unadjusted Cost	Inflation Multiplier		Adjusted Annual Total
2013	Jacob Hashimoto	Kites	Sculpture	$641,427	1.046	$670,932.64	$5,865,332.03
2013	Tim Rollins & K.O.S.	A Declaration of Conscience (after Senator Margaret Chase Smith)	Painting	$135,000	1.046	$141,210.00	
2013	Mark di Suvero	Thanks from the Saved Ones	Sculpture	$1,113,000	1.046	$1,164,198.00	
2013	Kimsooja	An Album: Sewing into Borderlines	Time-based media	$550,000	1.046	$575,300.00	
2013	Cliff Garten	Ribbons	Environmental art	$425,000	1.046	$444,550.00	
2013	Ellen Harvey	The Reforestation of the Andover IRS	Architectural arts	$225,000	1.046	$235,350.00	
2013	Tim Bavington	Louie Louie	Sculpture	$150,000	1.046	$156,900.00	
2013	Anne Lindberg	Curtain Wall	Architectural arts	$295,465	1.046	$309,056.39	
2013	Nina Katchadourian	Grand State of Maine	Sculpture	$145,000	1.046	$151,670.00	
2013	Teresita Fernandez	Nocturnal (Navigation)	Sculpture	$600,000	1.046	$627,600.00	
2013	Tsehai Johnson	Field Pattern	Sculpture	$100,000	1.046	$104,600.00	
2013	R. Scott Baltz	Opening Sky Stillness	Painting	$7,500	1.046	$7,845.00	
2013	R. Scott Baltz	Moving Sky Mirrored	Painting	$7,500	1.046	$7,845.00	

Year	Artist	Title	Classification	Unadjusted Cost	Inflation Multiplier		Adjusted Annual Total
2013	John Bisbee	Lion Dandies	Sculpture	$113,000	1.046	$118,198.00	
2013	Odili Donald Odita	Infinite Horizon	Painting	$175,000	1.046	$183,050.00	
2013	Kent Bloomer	(untitled)	Sculpture	$244,500	1.046	$255,747.00	
2013	Kim MacConnell	Intermission I	Painting	$100,000	1.046	$104,600.00	
2013	Kim MacConnell	Intermission II	Painting	$100,000	1.046	$104,600.00	
2013	An-My Lê	True Bearing	Photograph	$420,000	1.046	$439,320.00	
2013	Julie Moos	The New Americans	Photograph	$60,000	1.046	$62,760.00	
	Artist	**Title**	**Classification**	**Unadjusted Cost**	**Inflation Multiplier**		**Adjusted Annual Total**
2014	Matthew Ritchie	This Garden at This Hour	Environmental art	$600,000	1.029	$617,400.00	$3,683,721.22
2014	James Carpenter	Suspended Light Pillars	Sculpture	$400,000	1.029	$411,600.00	
2014	Vera Lutter	Forest	Sculpture	$150,000	1.029	$154,350.00	
2014	Spencer Finch	Glacial Erratic (New England)	Drawing	$163,110	1.029	$167,840.19	
2014	Meejin Yoon	Double Horizon	Time-based media	$562,000	1.029	$578,298.00	
2014	Mary Temple	Winter Light	Architectural arts	$160,000	1.029	$164,640.00	
2014	Matthew Moore	Passage	Sculpture	$250,000	1.029	$257,250.00	
2014	Eric Sall	RBFB Tower	Painting	$77,622	1.029	$79,873.04	
2014	Leonardo Drew	Number 123	Sculpture	$160,000	1.029	$164,640.00	
2014	Andrea Zittel	Planar Pavilion for the Denver Federal Center	Environmental art	$582,172	1.029	$599,054.99	
2014	Monica Ponce de Leon	Woven Voices	Sculpture	$150,000	1.029	$154,350.00	
2014	Simparch	Rodadora Frontera	Sculpture	$325,000	1.029	$334,425.00	
	Artist	**Title**	**Classification**	**Unadjusted Cost**	**Inflation Multiplier**		**Adjusted Annual Total**
2015	Inigo Manglano-Ovalle	Prototype for Re-Entry	Sculpture	$750,000	1.028	$771,000.00	$2,701,070.00
2015	Monica Ponce de Leon	Down River	Sculpture	$45,000	1.028	$46,260.00	
2015	Liz Larner	Public Jewel	Sculpture	$434,000	1.028	$446,152.00	
2015	Norie Sato	Of a Leaf or a Feather	Sculpture	$350,000	1.028	$359,800.00	
2015	Ursula von Rydingsvard	Cedrus	Sculpture	$750,000	1.028	$771,000.00	
2015	Mark Dion	Pantheon	Sculpture	$298,500	1.028	$306,858.00	
	Artist	**Title**	**Classification**	**Unadjusted Cost**	**Inflation Multiplier**		**Adjusted Annual Total**
2016	Catherine Opie	Yosemite Falls	Photograph	$500,000	1.015	$507,500.00	$1,522,500.00
2016	Mary Corse	Untitled (White Black Red Yellow Blue)	Painting	$500,000	1.015	$507,500.00	
2016	Gary Simmons	Mural	Painting	$500,000	1.015	$507,500.00	
	TOTAL	**AVG**	**Standard Deviation**	**1SD**	**2SD**	**3SD**	
	$90,118,908.66	$160,639.77	$363,924.29	$567,208.81	$727,848.58	$888,488.35	

FIGURE 4.1   EACH ART IN ARCHITECTURE COMMISSION, ADJUSTED

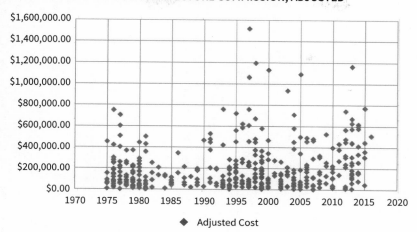

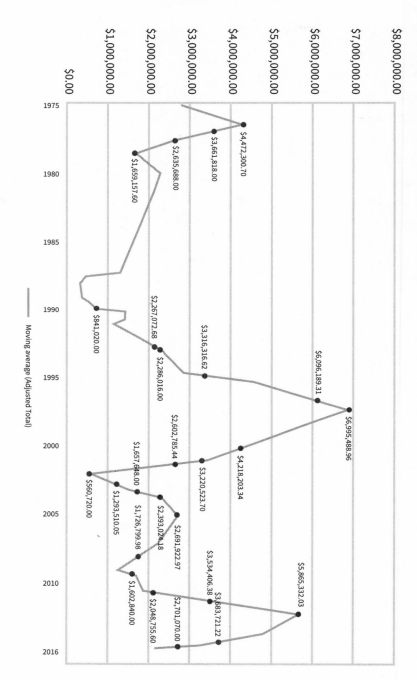

FIGURE 4.2   TOTAL AIA ACQUISITION PRICE BY YEAR

List of Abbreviations

APP Art in Public Places
ELO Eisenhower Legacy Organization
EMC Eisenhower Memorial Commission
EWAI Eisenhower World Affairs Institute
FBI Federal Bureau of Investigation
FOH Federal Occupational Health
FOIA Freedom of Information Act
FY Fiscal Year
GSA General Services Administration
ICA Institute of Contemporary Art
NCPC National Capitol Planning Commission
NEA National Endowment for the Arts
NEH National Endowment for the Humanities
PBS Public Buildings Services
RAO Regional Arts Organization
RFAO Regional Fine Arts Officer
RFQ Request for Quotation
SECCA Southeastern Center for Contemporary Art
TEB Technical Evaluation Board
VARA Visual Artists Rights Act

Notes

INTRODUCTION

1 Tracy Kamerer and Scott Nolley, "Rediscovering an American Icon: Houdon's Washington," *Colonial Williamsburg Journal*, Autumn 2003, http://www.history.org/Foundation/journal/Autumn03/houdon.cfm.

2 Sarah Cascone, "A Treasure Hunt for Lost WPA Paintings," *Artnet News*, April 22, 2014, https://news.artnet.com/art-world/a-treasure-hunt-for-lost-wpa-masterpieces-11376.

CHAPTER 1: THE EISENHOWER MEMORIAL

1 "Department of Defense Appropriations Act, 2000," Pub. L. No. 106–79, § 8162, 113 STAT. 1275 (1999), https://www.congress.gov/bill/106th-congress/house-bill/2561?q=%7B%22search%22%3A%5B%22H.R.+2561%22%5D%7D&r=1.

2 "Dwight D. Eisenhower Memorial Commission Meeting, April 26, 2001" (Dwight D. Eisenhower Memorial Commission, approved July 9, 2001), 3, http://www.eisenhowermemorial.org/sites/default/files/public/minutes/010426__2001%20April%2026_Approved%20Commission%20Meeting%20Minutes.pdf.

3 "Dwight D. Eisenhower Memorial Commission Meeting, September 12, 2002" (Dwight D. Eisenhower Memorial Commission, approved June 11, 2003), 2, www.eisenhowermemorial.org/sites/default/files/public/minutes/020912__2002%20September%2012_Approved%20Commission%20Meeting%20Minutes.pdf.

4 "Dwight D. Eisenhower Memorial Commission Meeting, February 28, 2002" (Dwight D. Eisenhower Memorial Commission, approved April 25, 2002), 4, http://www.eisenhowermemorial.org/sites/default/files/public/minutes/020228__2002%20February%2028_Approved%20Commission%20Meeting%20Minutes.pdf.

5 ""Dwight D. Eisenhower Memorial Commission Meeting, June 11, 2003" (Dwight D. Eisenhower Memorial Commission, approved March 25, 2004), 3, http://www.eisenhowermemorial.org/sites/default/files/public/minutes/030611_2003%20June%2011_Approved%20Commission%20Meeting%20Minutes.pdf.

6 "Dwight D. Eisenhower Memorial Commission Meeting, June 11, 2003," 3.

7 "Dwight D. Eisenhower Memorial Commission Meeting, June 11, 2003," 8.

8 "Oversight Hearing on 'The Proposed Dwight D. Eisenhower Memorial,'" § Committee on Natural Resources, Subcommittee on National Parks, Forests, and Public Lands (2012), 18, https://www.gpo.gov/fdsys/pkg/CHRG-112hhrg73488/pdf/CHRG-112hhrg73488.pdf.

9 "Dwight D. Eisenhower Memorial Commission Meeting, June 11, 2003,"3.

10 "Dwight D. Eisenhower Memorial Commission FY 2015 Budget Justification." http://www.eisenhowermemorial.org/sites/default/files/public/budget/FY2015%20Budget%20Justification_0.pdf

11 "Oversight Hearing on 'The Proposed Dwight D. Eisenhower Memorial,'" 18.

12 "Dwight D. Eisenhower Memorial Commission Meeting, April 26, 2001," 3.

13 "Dwight D. Eisenhower Memorial Commission Meeting, March 9, 2005" (Dwight D. Eisenhower Memorial Commission, approved June 20, 2005), 7, http://www.eisenhowermemorial.org/sites/default/files/public/minutes/050309_2005%20March%209_Approved%20Commission%20Meeting%20Minutes.pdf.

14 "The Art of Memorial Design Competitions," *Washington Post*, March 13, 2014, sec. Letters to the Editor, https://www.washingtonpost.com/opinions/the-art-of-memorial-design-competitions/2014/03/13/a353a2f6-aa08-11e3-8a7b-c1c684e2671f_story.html.

15 "The J. Paul Getty Trust," About the Getty, accessed February 6, 2018, http://www.getty.edu/about/governance/trustees.html.

16 "Thomas Jefferson Memorial," National Park Service, U.S. Department of the Interior, accessed February 6, 2018, https://www.nps.gov/nr/travel/presidents/thomas_jefferson_memorial.html.

17 Jimmy Stamp, "The Failed Attempt to Design a Memorial for Franklin Roosevelt," *Smithsonian Magazine*, July 22, 2014, last modified July 23, 2014, https://www.smithsonianmag.com/arts-culture/eisenhower-memorial-complications-recall-marcel-breuers-unbuilt-roosevelt-memorial-180952096/.

18 "Design Competition," National World War II Memorial, accessed

February 6, 2018, http://www.wwiimemorial.com/archives/factsheets/design_competition.htm?thispage=factsheet.

19 Megan Gambino, "Building the Martin Luther King, Jr. National Memorial," *Smithsonian Magazine*, August 18, 2011, https://www.smithsonianmag.com/history/building-the-martin-luther-king-jr-national-memorial-54721785/.

20 "Over 350 Entries in World War One Memorial Design Competition," The United States World War One Centennial Commission, August 5, 2015, http://www.worldwar1centennial.org/index.php/communicate/press-media/wwi-centennial-news/656-over-350-entries-in-world-war-one-memorial-design-competition.html.

21 Although the design competition for the National World War II Memorial was also overseen by GSA, that competition received more than four hundred design concepts and, importantly, noted that the criteria for selection were "on their originality, appropriateness, feasibility, and compliance with project requirements." See "Design Competition," World War II Memorial Factsheet, National World War II Memorial, www.wwiimemorial.com/archives/factsheets/design_competition.htm?thispage=factsheet.

22 "Dwight D. Eisenhower Memorial Commission Congressional Budget Justification, Fiscal Year 2015."

23 "Design Excellence in Public Design Contract Announcement" (General Services Administration, n.d.): 1, https://www.competitionline.com/upload/downloads/10xx/1087_13863_eisenhower.pdf.

24 "Oversight Hearing on 'The Proposed Dwight D. Eisenhower Memorial,'" 46.

25 "Design Excellence in Public Design Contract Announcement."

26 It is worth noting that both Robert Ivy, an architect, and David Eisenhower served on both this blind jury and the Design Excellence board, the final authority on architect selection.

27 "Jury Report: Dwight D. Eisenhower Memorial, Stage III Design Vision," U.S. General Services Administration (March 18, 2009), quoted in "A Five-Star Folly: An Investigation into the Cost Increases, Construction Delays, and Design Problems That Have Been a Disservice to the Effort to Memorialize Dwight D. Eisenhower," Majority Staff Report (Washington, DC: Committee on Natural Resources, Office of Oversight and Investigations, U.S. House of Representatives, 113th Congress, July 25, 2014): 19, https://naturalresources.house.gov/uploadedfiles/oversightreport-113-eisenhowermemorial.pdf.

28 "Oversight Hearing on 'The Proposed Dwight D. Eisenhower Memorial,'" 19.

29 Ibid.

30 "A Five-Star Folly," 15.

31 Charles Jencks, ed., *Frank O. Gehry: Individual Imagination and Cultural Conservatism* (New York: Wiley, 1995), 33.

32 Feil reportedly received more than $1.7 million in salary between 2005 and 2013, in addition to having his parking fees and internet access covered by taxpayers. "A Five-Star Folly," 25.

33 Bob Thompson, "Corcoran Director Quits; Trustees Shelve Gehry Plans," *Washington Post*, May 24, 2005, http://www.washingtonpost. com/wp-dyn/content/article/2005/05/23/AR2005052301838.html. Carol Vogel, "Corcoran Gallery's President Resigns in Dispute over Proposed Expansion," *New York Times*, May 25, 2005, http://www. nytimes.com/2005/05/25/arts/design/corcoran-gallerys-president-resigns-in-dispute-over-proposed.html.

34 Quoted in Thompson, "Corcoran Director Quits."

35 Quoted in ibid.

36 Luke Mullins, "Crisis at the Corcoran," *Washingtonian*, December 2012, posted November 27, 2012, https://www.washingtonian. com/2012/11/27/crisis-at-the-corcoran/.

37 "Dwight D. Eisenhower Memorial Commission Meeting, March 31, 2009" (Dwight D. Eisenhower Memorial Commission, approved March 25, 2010), 5, http://www.eisenhowermemorial.org/sites/default/ files/public/minutes/090331_2009%20March%2031_Approved%20 Commission%20Meeting%20Minutes.pdf.

38 *"Dwight D. Eisenhower Memorial—Our Thoughts on Eisenhower and His Memorial,"* Gehry Partners, LLP, at 1:44 (March 2009), quoted in "A Five-Star Folly."

39 "Dwight D. Eisenhower Memorial Commission Meeting - March 25, 2010" (Dwight D. Eisenhower Memorial Commission, approved July 12, 2011), 2, http://www.eisenhowermemorial.org/sites/default/ files/public/minutes/100325_2010%20March%2025_Approved%20 Commission%20Meeting%20Minutes.pdf.

40 Ibid., 4.

41 Ibid.

42 "A Five-Star Folly," 38.

43 "Oversight Hearing on 'The Proposed Dwight D. Eisenhower Memorial.'" 16.

44 Philip Kennicott, "Review: Frank Gehry's Eisenhower Memorial Reinvigorates the Genre," *Washington Post*, December 15, 2011, sec. Style, https://www.washingtonpost.com/lifestyle/style/review-frank-gehrys-eisenhower-memorial-reinvigorates-the-genre/2011/12/13/ gIQAAT4RwO_story.html.

45 Bruce Cole, "A Monumental Shame," *New Criterion*, December 2014, https://www.newcriterion.com/issues/2014/12/a-monumental-shame.

46 "Oversight Hearing on 'The Proposed Dwight D. Eisenhower Memorial,'" 20.

47 John Hawkinson, "MIT Settles with Gehry over Stata Ctr. Defects," *The Tech*, March 19, 2010, https://thetech.com/2010/03/19/statasuit-v130-n14.

48 Quoted in Robin Pogrebin and Katie Zezima, "M.I.T. Sues Frank Gehry, Citing Flaws in Center He Designed," *New York Times*, November 7, 2007, http://www.nytimes.com/2007/11/07/us/07mit.html.

49 "Oversight Hearing on 'The Proposed Dwight D. Eisenhower Memorial,'" 16.

50 "Students See Inside Politics Firsthand," Eisenhower Institute at Gettysburg College, accessed February 6, 2018, http://www.eisenhowerinstitute.org/news/news_detail.dot?inode=2478c532-270b-48de-83fb-0ca7a543469c&pageTitle=Students%2Bsee%2BInside%2BPolitics%2Bfirsthand. "Dwight D. Eisenhower Memorial Commission Salary Statistics," accessed February 14, 2018, https://www.federalpay.org/employees/dwight-d-eisenhower-memorial-commission/2008.

51 "Dwight D. Eisenhower Memorial Commission Salary Statistics."

52 Even after 2008, when the Commission began to hire full-time employees, persons like executive architect Dan Feil continued to receive funding from another source, so the amounts listed above do not cover full salary expenditures from the Eisenhower Memorial Commission.

53 Hannah Hess, "House Subcommittee Votes to Eliminate Funds for Eisenhower Memorial," *Roll Call*, July 9, 2014, http://www.rollcall.com/news/home/eisenhower-memorial-in-trouble.

54 Hannah Hess, "National Capital Planning Commission Rejects Frank Gehry's Design for Eisenhower Memorial," *Roll Call*, April 7, 2014, https://www.rollcall.com/news/national-capital-planning-commission-rejects-frank-gehrys-design-for-eisenhower-memorial.

55 "A Five-Star Folly," 54.

56 Fred Barbash, "GOP Congressional Report: Eisenhower Memorial a 'Five-Star Folly,'" *Washington Post*, August 4, 2014, sec. Morning Mix, https://www.washingtonpost.com/news/morning-mix/wp/2014/08/04/gop-congressional-report-eisenhower-memorial-a-five-star-folly/.

57 "A Five-Star Folly," 1.

58 Ibid.The Commemorative Works Act was passed as a means of keeping the National Capital Area from becoming oversaturated with monuments. Originally passed in 1986 and amended several

times since, the Commemorative Works Act requires that proposed memorials receive final design approval from the National Capital Planning Commission and the Commission of Fine Arts, as well as all construction funds in hand, before construction begins.

59 "Dwight D. Eisenhower Memorial Commission Meeting, February 28, 2002" (Dwight D. Eisenhower Memorial Commission, approved April 25, 2002), 4, http://www.eisenhowermemorial.org/sites/default/ files/public/minutes/020228_2002%20February%2028_Approved%20 Commission%20Meeting%20Minutes.pdf.

60 "Dwight D. Eisenhower Memorial Commission Meeting, July 26, 2007" (Dwight D. Eisenhower Memorial Commission, approved March 31, 2009), 3, http://www.eisenhowermemorial.org/sites/default/ files/public/minutes/070726_2007%20July%2026_Approved%20 Commission%20Meeting%20Minutes.pdf.

61 "A Five-Star Folly," 29.

62 Ibid, 30.

63 Ibid.

64 "Dwight D. Eisenhower Memorial Commission Meeting, March 25, 2010," 7.

65 Hannah Hess, "Eisenhower Memorial Losing Support from Congress," *Roll Call*, January 15, 2014, https://www.rollcall.com/news/ eisenhower_memorial_losing_support_from_congress-230195-1. html.

66 "A Five-Star Folly," 32.

67 Ibid.

68 Nathan Rubbelke, "Controversial Design for Eisenhower Memorial Approved," *Washington Examiner*, July 9, 2015, http://www. washingtonexaminer.com/controversial-design-for-eisenhower- memorial-approved/article/2567968.

69 "Dwight D. Eisenhower Memorial Commission Meeting, April 29, 2015" (Dwight D. Eisenhower Memorial Commission, approved December 1, 2016), 1, http://www.eisenhowermemorial.org/sites/ default/files/public/minutes/161201_150429%20Commission%20 Meeting%20Minutes_Approved.pdf.

70 Hannah Hess, "Pat Roberts: 'Nothing Less than Full Victory' on Ike Memorial," *Roll Call*, April 29, 2015, http://www.rollcall.com/news/ home/pat-roberts-nothing-less-than-full-victory-on-ike-memorial.

71 Rocco Siciliano, a 2012 letter to Senator Inouye, quoted in Carol Ross Joynt, "Tug of War," *Washingtonian*, May 2014, posted April 30, 2014, https://www.washingtonian.com/2014/04/30/tug-of-war/.

72 Bob Dole, "What's the Matter With Kansas? 'Not a Damn Thing' | Letter to the Editor," *Roll Call*, August 7, 2015, https://www.rollcall. com/news/bob-dole-ike-memorial-letter-to-the-editor.

73 Graham Bowley, "Eisenhower Family Drops Objections to Memorial," *New York Times*, September 19, 2016, sec. Art & Design, https://www.nytimes.com/2016/09/20/arts/design/eisenhower-family-drops-objections-to-memorial.html.

74 Michelle Goldchain, "Eisenhower Family Finally Supports Frank Gehry's Eisenhower Memorial," *Curbed DC* (blog), September 21, 2016, https://dc.curbed.com/2016/9/21/13000868/eisenhower-memorial-frank-gehry.

75 "Oversight Hearing on 'The Proposed Dwight D. Eisenhower Memorial,'" 16.

76 "The revised preliminary plans eliminated the east and west tapestries and proposed two freestanding columns as a replacement to define the memorial space." See "Executive Director's Recommendation" (National Capital Planning Commission, February 2, 2017): 6, https://www.ncpc.gov/docs/actions/2017February/Eisenhower_Memorial_Modification_Recommendation_6694_Feb2017.pdf.

77 Ibid.

78 "Final Determination of Effect, Stipulation 11 of the 2012 Memorandum of Agreement" (National Park Service, September 8, 2017): 8, attachment from https://parkplanning.nps.gov/document.cfm?parkID=427&projectID=16139&documentID=82757.

79 Catesby Leigh, "A Monumental Folly," *City Journal*, May 26, 2017, https://www.city-journal.org/html/monumental-folly-15219.html.

80 "Who We Are | Commission of Fine Arts," U.S. Commission of Fine Arts, accessed February 6, 2018, https://www.cfa.gov/about-cfa/who-we-are.

81 Griffin Connolly, "Eisenhower Memorial Clears Key Construction Hurdle," *Roll Call*, September 21, 2017, sec. Politics, https://www.rollcall.com/news/politics/eisenhower-memorial-clears-key-hurdle-construction.

82 Peggy McGlone, "With Groundbreaking, Elusive Eisenhower Memorial Moves from Dream to Reality," *Washington Post,* October 31, 2017, https://www.washingtonpost.com/entertainment/museums/with-groundbreaking-elusive-eisenhower-memorial-moves-from-dream-to-reality/2017/10/31/d37477c4-be56-11e7-97d9-bdab5a0ab381_story.html?utm_term=.688c78a1c3e4.

CHAPTER 2: ART IN ARCHITECTURE

1 "Introductory Panel Meeting - FBI Building, Miramar, Florida" (General Services Administration, August 24, 2010), 2, https://foiaonline.regulations.gov/foia/action/public/view/record?objectId=090004d28130785a.

2 Ibid, 4.

3 "Artist Selection Meeting - FBI Building, Miramar, Florida" (General Services Administration, November 5, 2010), 2, https://foiaonline. regulations.gov/foia/action/public/view/record?objectId=090004d2813 0785a, from FOIA file.

4 "Technical Evaluation of Artists - FBI District Office, Miramar, Florida" (General Services Administration, April 14, 2011), 6, https:// foiaonline.regulations.gov/foia/action/public/view/record?objectId=09 0004d28130785a, from FOIA file.

5 For example, in the technical evaluations for a commission in Yuma, Arizona, one artist received a score of 8 for "Past Performance" despite glowing reviews from his three recommenders, while another received a 9 for the same category despite one recommender stating that "his weakness is paperwork and . . . he might need a little extra help navigating the administrative aspects of managing a complex project (i.e. paperwork, schedule, etc.)." The second artist received the commission.

6 "Final Concept Review - Ursula von Rydingsvard" (General Services Administration, February 4, 2014), https://foiaonline.regulations.gov/ foia/action/public/view/record?objectId=090004d28130785a, from FOIA file.

7 In addition to being virtually indistinguishable from a half dozen other works by Von Rydingsvard, *Cedrus* is remarkably similar to an earlier Art in Architecture commission, Ming Fay's *Pillar Arc*, a cast iron work modeled on a "single scale of a cedar cone."

8 Matt Dixon, "$750K Sculpture Sickened FBI Workers in Miami," *Politico Florida*, December 2, 2016, https://www.politico.com/states/ florida/story/2016/12/the-750k-sculpture-that-hospitalized-fbi-miami-workers-107768.

9 Karen Michel, "When Sculpting Cedar, This Artist Is Tireless And Unsentimental," *NPR.Org*, April 28, 2013, https://www.npr. org/2013/04/28/177969148/when-sculpting-cedar-this-artist-is-tireless-and-unsentimental.

10 Eric Meier, "Wood Allergies and Toxicity," The Wood Database, www. wood-database.com/wood-articles/wood-allergies-and-toxicity/#npc.

11 Richard Haley to Norman Dong, January 29, 2016, https://foiaonline. regulations.gov/foia/action/public/view/record?objectId=090004d280a 5e7f6&fromSearch=true, from FOIA file.

12 Jennifer Gibson to Norman Dong, "Removal of Artwork," October 2, 2015, GSA-2016-000160, FOIA Online, https://foiaonline.regulations. gov/foia/action/public/view/record?objectId=090004d280a5e7f6&from Search=true.

13 Michael Goodwin to Sabina Sims, "Re: Path Forward Regarding Art

Sculpture in Miramar," July 30, 2015, https://foiaonline.regulations. gov/foia/action/public/view/record?objectId=090004d280a5e7f6&from Search=true, from FOIA file.

14 Haley to Dong, January 29, 2016, from FOIA file.

15 Richard Serra and Clara Weyergraf, *Richard Serra: Interviews, Etc. 1970–1980* (Yonkers, NY: Hudson River Museum, 1980), 128.

16 Michael Brenson, "Art View: The Messy Saga of 'Tilted Arc' Is Far from Over," *New York Times*, April 2, 1989, http://www.nytimes. com/1989/04/02/arts/art-view-the-messy-saga-of-tilted-arc-is-far- from-over.html.

17 "Visual Artists Rights Act of 1990," Pub. L. No. 101–650, 17 U.S. Code § 106A (1990).

18 Furthermore, Serra's claim of site-specificity would not be protected by VARA; site-specific artwork may be moved without threat of lawsuit. *Phillips v. Pembroke Real Estate, Inc.*, 459 F.3d 128 (1st Cir. 2006).

19 Quoted in "Golden Fleece Awards, 1975–1987," Wisconsin Historical Society, accessed February 7, 2018, http://content.wisconsinhistory. org/cdm/ref/collection/tp/id/70852.

20 Daniel Patrick Moynihan, "Guiding Principles for Federal Architecture," 1962, https://www.gsa.gov/real-estate/design- construction/design-excellence/design-excellence-program/guiding- principles-for-federal-architecture.

21 "Introductory Essay," in *GSA Art in Architecture: Selected Artworks 1997–2008* (Washington, DC: General Services Administration, 2008), 10.

22 Ibid., 22.

23 Ibid.

24 The only mention of the Art in Architecture program in Congress since 1993 appears to be an effort by Rep. Tim Griffin to pass through the "Hometown Artists Act of 2011," a bill that would have given preference to local artists for Art in Architecture commissions. The bill failed to pass the House.

25 "GSA Art in Architecture Policies and Procedures," General Services Administration (November 2010), 2, https://www.gsa.gov/cdnstatic/ AIA_policies_and_procedures.pdf.

26 Judith Resnik and Dennis Edward Curtis, *Representing Justice: Invention, Controversy, and Rights in City-States and Democratic Courtrooms* (New Haven, CT: Yale University Press, 2011), 191.

27 According to Steven J. Tepper, there were three distinct selection processes that evolved between 1972 and 1999. The selection process that was in place at the time of his publication (1999), however, seems

to have been dismantled sometime between 1999 and 2010; apparently
the selection process immediately after the GSA-NEA split included
ten-person panels (with five art professionals and five "citizens and
community leaders"), but the selection panel at present is made up of
only seven people. Steven J. Tepper, "Unfamiliar Objects in Familiar
Spaces: The Public Response to Art-in-Architecture," in *Center for
Arts and Cultural Policy Studies, Princeton University* (1999), posted
March 2, 1999, https://www.issuelab.org/resource/unfamiliar-objects-
in-familiar-spaces-the-public-response-to-art-in-architecture.html.

28 "GSA Art in Architecture Policies and Procedures," 5.

29 Ibid., 8.

30 Ibid., 9.

31 Ibid., 9.

32 Ibid., 10.

33 Ibid., 5.

34 Ibid., 3.

35 Ibid., 11.

36 Ibid., 13.

37 Ibid., 12.

38 Ibid., 13.

39 Ibid., 13.

40 Ibid., 15.

41 Ibid., 16.

42 Ibid.

43 Ibid., 17.

44 Ibid.

45 Ibid., 18.

46 Michael Miller, "The Dog-Killing Woes of Tom Otterness," *Observer*
(blog), October 4, 2011, http://observer.com/2011/10/the-dog-killing-
woes-of-tom-otterness/.

47 Tyler Getter, "Art Inspection Form - Christopher Sproat, Untitled"
(Fine Arts Program, General Services Administration, September 21,
2016), https://foiaonline.regulations.gov/foia/action/public/view/reque
st?objectId=090004d28105119b, from FOIA file.

48 Jo Ann Lewis, "Showdown on 'Hoe-Down,'" *Washington Post*,
September 26, 1979, https://www.washingtonpost.com/archive/
lifestyle/1979/09/26/showdown-on-hoe-down/b69215d6-5a18-42cf-
bc62-34d692a90d8a/?utm_term=.e3af30331902.

49 "Technical Evaluation of Artists - Calais, Maine Land Port of Entry,"
August 29, 2006, https://foiaonline.regulations.gov/foia/action/public/
view/record?objectId=090004d28130785a, from FOIA file.

50 "Minutes for Third Panel Meeting - Calais, Maine Land Port of

Entry" (General Services Administration, July 19, 2007), 1, https://foiaonline.regulations.gov/foia/action/public/view/record?objectId=090004d28130785a, from FOIA file.

51 "Final Concept Review - Buster Simpson" (General Services Administration, June 15, 2011), https://foiaonline.regulations.gov/foia/action/public/view/record?objectId=090004d28130785a, 1–2, from FOIA file.

52 "Where's the Art?," General Services Administration, accessed February 9, 2018, https://www.gsa.gov/real-estate/gsa-properties/visiting-public-buildings/gsa-headquarters-building/whats-inside/wheres-the-art.

53 Ibid.

54 GSA, *Planar Pavilion, Denver Federal Center, Lakewood, Colorado* (General Services Administration, September 29, 2016), https://www.youtube.com/watch?v=ykcfSzMV7WQ, at :57.

55 GSA, *Planar Pavilion*, at 1:15.

56 "Thanks from the Saved Ones," GSA Fine Arts Collection, accessed February 9, 2018, https://www.gsa.gov/fine-arts#/artwork/26063.

57 Ibid.

58 M. H. Miller, "A Contemporary Art Titan's (Almost) Secret Commune," *New York Times*, October 27, 2016, sec. T–Style magazine, https://www.nytimes.com/2016/10/27/t-magazine/art/mark-di-suvero-socrates-sculpture-park.html.

59 "Final Artist's Concept Presentation for 50 UN Plaza" (General Services Administration, May 28, 2010), 4, https://foiaonline.regulations.gov/foia/action/public/view/record?objectId=090004d28130785a, from FOIA file.

60 "Minutes for Final Proposal Presentation, Conference Call with Gary Simmons" (General Services Administration, September 30, 2015), 11, https://foiaonline.regulations.gov/foia/action/public/view/record?objectId=090004d28130785a, from FOIA file.

61 "Final Concept Review- Odili Donald Odita" (General Services Administration, June 27, 2013), 8, https://foiaonline.regulations.gov/foia/action/public/view/record?objectId=090004d28130785a, from FOIA file.

62 Ibid.

CHAPTER 3: THE NATIONAL ENDOWMENT FOR THE ARTS

1 "2017: WALLS," San Francisco Mime Troupe—America's Theater of Political Comedy, accessed February 9, 2018, http://www.sfmt.org/company/archives/walls/2017.php.

2 Gia Kourlas, "But Is It Art? In the Case of 'Doggie Hamlet,' Yes," *New*

York Times, April 7, 2017, https://www.nytimes.com/2017/04/07/arts/
dance/but-is-it-art-in-the-case-of-doggie-hamlet-yes.html?mtrref=un
defined&gwh=9653829FD2F24EBC73BBE90B765E3645&gwt=pay.

3 "National Foundation on the Arts and the Humanities Act of 1965,"
   Pub. L. No. 89-209, S. 1483 845 (1965), https://www.gpo.gov/fdsys/pkg/
   STATUTE-79/pdf/STATUTE-79-Pg845.pdf.

4 "Lyndon B. Johnson: Remarks at the Signing of the Arts and
   Humanities Bill," The American Presidency Project, accessed
   February 12, 2018, http://www.presidency.ucsb.edu/ws/?pid=27279.
   The "vision . . . perish" reference is citing the biblical book of
   Proverbs (29:18).

5 "H. Rept. 104-170—Arts, Humanities, and Museum Services
   Amendments of 1995," legislation (Washington, DC: United States
   House of Representatives, June 29, 1995), https://www.congress.gov/
   congressional-report/104th-congress/house-report/170/1.

6 Mark Bauerlein, ed., *National Endowment for the Arts: A History,
   1965–2008* (Washington, DC: National Endowment for the Arts, 2009),
   22.

7 Ronald Lee Fleming, "Public Art for the Public," *The Public Interest*,
   March 2005, http://www.nationalaffairs.com/storage/app/uploads/publ
   ic/58e/1a5/093/58e1a509377f7647325678.pdf, 61.

8 Liz Stark Auclair, "Art Out Loud: Public Art Takes Over DC," *NEA
   Arts Magazine* 2010, no. 2, https://www.arts.gov/NEARTS/2010v2-
   arts-capital/art-out-loud; Donna M. Binkiewicz, *Federalizing the
   Muse: United States Arts Policy and the National Endowment for the
   Arts, 1965–1980* (Chapel Hill: University of North Carolina Press,
   2004), 140.

9 Quoted in Garret Ellison, "Inherently Controversial: How Grand
   Rapids Got a Calder Sculpture in the First Place," MLive.com,
   October 6, 2013, updated June 2, 2016, http://www.mlive.com/news/
   grand-rapids/index.ssf/2013/10/artprize_2013_is_hardly_calder.html.

10 Quoted in ibid.

11 Quoted in ibid.

12 Bauerlein, *National Endowment for the Arts*, 27.

13 Andres Serrano, "Protecting Freedom of Expression, from Piss Christ
    to Charlie Hebdo," *Creative Time Reports*, January 30, 2015, http://
    creativetime.org/reports/2015/01/30/free-speech-piss-christ-charlie-
    hebdo-andres-serrano/.

14 Bauerlein, *National Endowment for the Arts*, 116.

15 Quoted in Travis M. Andrews, "Behind the Right's Loathing of the
    NEA: Two 'Despicable' Exhibits Almost 30 Years Ago," *Washington
    Post*, March 20, 2017, sec. Morning Mix, https://www.washingtonpost.

com/news/morning-mix/wp/2017/03/20/behind-the-loathing-of-the-national-endowment-for-the-arts-a-pair-of-despicable-exhibits-almost-30-years-ago/.

16 Quoted in Fleming, "Public Art for the Public," 62.

17 "Art Works Guidelines: We Fund/We Do Not Fund," National Endowment for the Arts, accessed February 12, 2018, https://www.arts.gov/grants-organizations/art-works/we-fund-we-do-not-fund.

18 Bryan Manabat, "Arts Council Not Eligible for NEA Funds until 2018," *Marianas Variety*, April 15, 2016, http://www.mvariety.com/cnmi/cnmi-news/local/85407-arts-council-not-eligible-for-nea-funds-until-2018.

19 "Illinois," Americans for the Arts, June 29, 2017, www.americansforthearts.org/by-location/illinois.

20 Individual Artist Program, Indiana Arts Commission, www.in.gov/arts/files/FY18-IAP.pdf.

21 "Grants for Artists," Mid Atlantic Arts Foundation (MAAF), www.midatlanticarts.org/grants-programs/grants-for-artists/#state-fellowships.

22 "Funders," New England Foundation for the Arts, accessed February 12, 2018, https://www.nefa.org/about_us/funders.

23· "New US Embassy in Islamabad to Get $400,000 Camel Sculpture," *Express Tribune*, March 31, 2014, https://tribune.com.pk/story/689550/new-us-embassy-in-islamabad-to-get-400000-camel-sculpture/.

24 "29 Pieces, Dallas, TX," NEA Online Grant Search, accessed February 12, 2018, https://apps.nea.gov/GrantSearch/.

25 Lisa Boykin Batts, "NEA Support Boosted Whirligig Park," *Wilson Times*, March 30, 2017, http://www.wilsontimes.com/stories/nea-support-boosted-whirligig-park,82953.

26 "Vollis Simpson Whirligig Park (Wilson)," accessed February 15, 2018, https://www.tripadvisor.com/Attraction_Review-g49674-d8698153-Reviews-Vollis_Simpson_Whirligig_Park-Wilson_North_Carolina.html.

27 "Arts and Artifacts Indemnity Program," National Endowment for the Arts, June 2017, https://www.arts.gov/artistic-fields/museums/arts-and-artifacts-indemnity-program-international-indemnity.

28 Ibid.

29 Ibid.

30 Patricia Loiko to Joseph Studemeyer, "Recently Indemnified Exhibition Information Request," September 25, 2017.

31 "Walters Presents A Feast for the Senses: Art and Experience in Medieval Europe," The Walters Art Museum, October 6, 2016, https://thewalters.org/news/releases/article.aspx?e_id=517.

APPENDIX

1 All artwork, artist, and original cost data released by GSA January 20, 2017. Mary Margaret Carr, "Acquisition Cost - Installed Art in Architecture Works" (General Services Administration, January 5, 2017).

Bibliography

CHAPTER 1: THE EISENHOWER MEMORIAL

"A FIVE-STAR FOLLY: An Investigation into the Cost Increases, Construction Delays, and Design Problems That Have Been a Disservice to the Effort to Memorialize Dwight D. Eisenhower." Majority Staff Report. Washington, DC: Committee on Natural Resources, Office of Oversight and Investigations, U.S. House of Representatives, 113th Congress, July 25, 2014. https://naturalresources.house.gov/uploadedfiles/oversightreport-113-eisenhowermemorial.pdf.

Barbash, Fred. "GOP Congressional Report: Eisenhower Memorial a 'Five-Star Folly.'" *Washington Post*, August 4, 2014, sec. Morning Mix. https://www.washingtonpost.com/news/morning-mix/wp/2014/08/04/gop-congressional-report-eisenhower-memorial-a-five-star-folly/.

Bowley, Graham. "Eisenhower Family Drops Objections to Memorial." *New York Times*, September 19, 2016, sec. Art & Design. https://www.nytimes.com/2016/09/20/arts/design/eisenhower-family-drops-objections-to-memorial.html.

Cascone, Sarah. "A Treasure Hunt for Lost WPA Paintings." *Artnet News*, April 22, 2014. https://news.artnet.com/art-world/a-treasure-hunt-for-lost-wpa-masterpieces-11376.

Cole, Bruce. "A Monumental Shame." *The New Criterion*, December 2014. https://www.newcriterion.com/issues/2014/12/a-monumental-shame.

Connolly, Griffin. "Eisenhower Memorial Clears Key Construction
    Hurdle." *Roll Call*. September 21, 2017, sec. Politics. https://www.
    rollcall.com/news/politics/eisenhower-memorial-clears-key-
    hurdle-construction.
Department of Defense Appropriations Act, 2000, Pub. L. No. 106–79,
    § 8162, 113 STAT. 1275 (1999). https://www.congress.gov/bill/106th-
    congress/house-bill/2561?q=%7B%22search%22%3A%5B%22H.R.+
    2561%22%5D%7D&r=1.
"Design Competition." National World War II Memorial. Accessed
    February 6, 2018. http://www.wwiimemorial.com/archives/
    factsheets/design_competition.htm?thispage=factsheet.
Dole, Bob. "What's the Matter with Kansas? 'Not a Damn Thing' |
    Letter to the Editor." *Roll Call*, August 7, 2015. https://www.rollcall.
    com/news/bob-dole-ike-memorial-letter-to-the-editor.
"Dwight D. Eisenhower Memorial Commission Congressional
    Budget Justification, Fiscal Year 2015," March 4, 2013. http://
    www.eisenhowermemorial.org/sites/default/files/public/budget/
    FY2015%20Budget%20Justification_0.pdf.
"Dwight D. Eisenhower Memorial Commission Meeting - April
    26, 2001." Dwight D. Eisenhower Memorial Commission, July
    9, 2001. http://www.eisenhowermemorial.org/sites/default/files/
    public/minutes/010426_2001%20April%2026_Approved%20
    Commission%20Meeting%20Minutes.pdf.
"Dwight D. Eisenhower Memorial Commission Meeting - April 29,
    2015." Dwight D. Eisenhower Memorial Commission, December
    1, 2016. http://www.eisenhowermemorial.org/sites/default/files/
    public/minutes/161201_150429%20Commission%20Meeting%20
    Minutes_Approved.pdf.
"Dwight D. Eisenhower Memorial Commission Meeting - February
    28, 2002." Dwight D. Eisenhower Memorial Commission, April
    25, 2002. http://www.eisenhowermemorial.org/sites/default/files/
    public/minutes/020228_2002%20February%2028_Approved%20
    Commission%20Meeting%20Minutes.pdf.
"Dwight D. Eisenhower Memorial Commission Meeting - July 26,
    2007." Dwight D. Eisenhower Memorial Commission, March
    31, 2009. http://www.eisenhowermemorial.org/sites/default/
    files/public/minutes/070726_2007%20July%2026_Approved%20
    Commission%20Meeting%20Minutes.pdf.
"Dwight D. Eisenhower Memorial Commission Meeting - June 11,
    2003." Dwight D. Eisenhower Memorial Commission, March

25, 2004. http://www.eisenhowermemorial.org/sites/default/
files/public/minutes/030611_2003%20June%2011_Approved%20
Commission%20Meeting%20Minutes.pdf.

"Dwight D. Eisenhower Memorial Commission Meeting - March
9, 2005." Dwight D. Eisenhower Memorial Commission, June
20, 2005. http://www.eisenhowermemorial.org/sites/default/files/
public/minutes/050309_2005%20March%209_Approved%20
Commission%20Meeting%20Minutes.pdf.

"Dwight D. Eisenhower Memorial Commission Meeting - March
25, 2010." Dwight D. Eisenhower Memorial Commission, July
12, 2011. http://www.eisenhowermemorial.org/sites/default/files/
public/minutes/100325_2010%20March%2025_Approved%20
Commission%20Meeting%20Minutes.pdf.

"Dwight D. Eisenhower Memorial Commission Meeting - March
31, 2009." Dwight D. Eisenhower Memorial Commission, March
25, 2010. http://www.eisenhowermemorial.org/sites/default/files/
public/minutes/090331_2009%20March%2031_Approved%20
Commission%20Meeting%20Minutes.pdf.

"Dwight D. Eisenhower Memorial Commission Meeting - September
12, 2002." Dwight D. Eisenhower Memorial Commission, June
11, 2003. www.eisenhowermemorial.org/sites/default/files/public/
minutes/020912_2002%20September%2012_Approved%20
Commission%20Meeting%20Minutes.pdf.

"Dwight D. Eisenhower Memorial Commission Salary Statistics."
Accessed February 14, 2018. https://www.federalpay.org/employees/
dwight-d-eisenhower-memorial-commission/2008.

Echoles, Bonnie. "Design Excellence in Public Design Contract
Announcement." General Services Administration, n.d. https://
www.competitionline.com/upload/downloads/10xx/1087_13863_
eisenhower.pdf.

"Executive Director's Recommendation." National Capitol Planning
Committee, February 2, 2017. https://www.ncpc.gov/docs/
actions/2017February/Eisenhower_Memorial_Modification_
Recommendation_6694_Feb2017.pdf.

"Final Determination of Effect, Stipulation 11 of the 2012
Memorandum of Agreement." National Park Service, September
18, 2017. https://parkplanning.nps.gov/document.cfm?parkID=427
&projectID=16139&documentID=82757.

Gambino, Megan. "Building the Martin Luther King, Jr.
National Memorial." *Smithsonian Magazine*. Accessed

February 6, 2018. https://www.smithsonianmag.com/history/
building-the-martin-luther-king-jr-national-memorial-54721785/.

Goldchain, Michelle. "Eisenhower Family Finally Supports
Frank Gehry's Eisenhower Memorial." *Curbed DC* (blog),
September 21, 2016. https://dc.curbed.com/2016/9/21/13000868/
eisenhower-memorial-frank-gehry.

Hawkinson, John. "MIT Settles with Gehry over Stata Ctr. Defects."
The Tech. March 19, 2010. https://thetech.com/2010/03/19/
statasuit-v130-n14.

Hess, Hannah. "Eisenhower Memorial Losing Support from
Congress." *Roll Call.* January 15, 2014. https://www.rollcall.
com/news/eisenhower_memorial_losing_support_from_
congress-230195-1.html.

———. "House Subcommittee Votes to Eliminate Funds for
Eisenhower Memorial." *Roll Call*, July 9, 2014. http://www.rollcall.
com/news/home/eisenhower-memorial-in-trouble.

———. "National Capital Planning Commission Rejects Frank
Gehry's Design for Eisenhower Memorial." *Roll Call*, April 7,
2014. https://www.rollcall.com/news/national-capital-planning-
commission-rejects-frank-gehrys-design-for-eisenhower-
memorial.

———. "Pat Roberts: 'Nothing Less than Full Victory' on Ike
Memorial." *Roll Call.* April 29, 2015. http://www.rollcall.com/news/
home/pat-roberts-nothing-less-than-full-victory-on-ike-memorial.

Jencks, Charles, ed. *Frank O. Gehry: Individual Imagination and
Cultural Conservatism.* 1st ed. London: New York: Wiley, 1995.

Joynt, Carol Ross. "Tug of War." *Washingtonian*, April 30, 2014. https://
www.washingtonian.com/2014/04/30/tug-of-war/.

Kamerer, Tracy, and Scott Nolley. "Rediscovering an American Icon:
Houdon's Washington." *The Colonial Williamsburg Journal*, Autumn
2003. http://www.history.org/Foundation/journal/Autumn03/
houdon.cfm.

Kennicott, Philip. "Review: Frank Gehry's Eisenhower Memorial
Reinvigorates the Genre." *Washington Post.* December 15, 2011,
sec. Style. https://www.washingtonpost.com/lifestyle/style/
review-frank-gehrys-eisenhower-memorial-reinvigorates-the-
genre/2011/12/13/gIQAAT4RwO_story.html.

Leigh, Catesby. "A Monumental Folly." *City Journal*, May 26, 2017.
https://www.city-journal.org/html/monumental-folly-15219.html.

McGlone, Peggy. "With Groundbreaking, Elusive Eisenhower
Memorial Moves from Dream to Reality," *Washington Post,*

October 31, 2017, https://www.washingtonpost.com/entertainment/
museums/with-groundbreaking-elusive-eisenhower-memorial-
moves-from-dream-to-reality/2017/10/31/d37477c4-be56-11e7-97d9-
bdab5a0ab381_story.html?utm_term=.688c78a1c3e4.

Mullins, Luke. "Crisis at the Corcoran." *Washingtonian*,
November 27, 2012. https://www.washingtonian.com/2012/11/27/
crisis-at-the-corcoran/.

"Over 350 Entries in World War One Memorial Design Competition."
The United States World War One Centennial Commission,
August 5, 2015. http://www.worldwar1centennial.org/index.php/
communicate/press-media/wwi-centennial-news/656-over-350-
entries-in-world-war-one-memorial-design-competition.html.

Oversight Hearing on "The Proposed Dwight D. Eisenhower
Memorial.," § Committee on Natural Resources, Subcommittee on
National Parks, Forests, and Public Lands (2012). https://www.gpo.
gov/fdsys/pkg/CHRG-112hhrg73488/pdf/CHRG-112hhrg73488.pdf.

Pogrebin, Robin, and Katie Zezima. "M.I.T. Sues Frank Gehry, Citing
Flaws in Center He Designed." *New York Times*. November 7, 2007.
http://www.nytimes.com/2007/11/07/us/07mit.html.

Rubbelke, Nathan. "Controversial Design for Eisenhower
Memorial Approved." *Washington Examiner*, July
9, 2015. http://www.washingtonexaminer.com/
controversial-design-for-eisenhower-memorial-approved/
article/2567968.

Stamp, Jimmy. "The Failed Attempt to Design a Memorial for
Franklin Roosevelt." *Smithsonian Magazine*. Accessed February 6,
2018. https://www.smithsonianmag.com/arts-culture/eisenhower-
memorial-complications-recall-marcel-breuers-unbuilt-roosevelt-
memorial-180952096/.

"Students See Inside Politics Firsthand." Eisenhower Institute at
Gettysburg College. Accessed February 6, 2018. http://www.
eisenhowerinstitute.org/news/news_detail.dot?inode=2478c532-
270b-48de-83fb-0ca7a543469c&pageTitle=Students%2Bsee%2BInsi
de%2BPolitics%2Bfirsthand.

"The Art of Memorial Design Competitions." *Washington Post*, March
13, 2014, sec. Letters to the Editor. https://www.washingtonpost.
com/opinions/the-art-of-memorial-design-competitions/2014/03/13/
a353a2f6-aa08-11e3-8a7b-c1c684e2671f_story.html.

"The J. Paul Getty Trust." About the Getty. Accessed February 6, 2018.
http://www.getty.edu/about/governance/trustees.html.

"Thomas Jefferson Memorial." National Park Service, U.S. Department of the Interior. Accessed February 6, 2018. https://www.nps.gov/nr/travel/presidents/thomas_jefferson_memorial.html.

Thompson, Bob. "Corcoran Director Quits; Trustees Shelve Gehry Plans." *Washington Post*, May 24, 2005. http://www.washingtonpost.com/wp-dyn/content/article/2005/05/23/AR2005052301838.html.

Vogel, Carol. "Corcoran Gallery's President Resigns in Dispute Over Proposed Expansion." *New York Times*. May 25, 2005. http://www.nytimes.com/2005/05/25/arts/design/corcoran-gallerys-president-resigns-in-dispute-over-proposed.html.

"Who We Are | Commission of Fine Arts." U.S. Commission of Fine Arts. Accessed February 6, 2018. https://www.cfa.gov/about-cfa/who-we-are.

CHAPTER 2: ART IN ARCHITECTURE

"Artist Selection Meeting - FBI Building, Miramar, Florida." General Services Administration, November 5, 2010. https://foiaonline.regulations.gov/foia/action/public/view/record?objectId=090004d28130785a.

Brenson, Michael. "ART VIEW; The Messy Saga of 'Tilted Arc' Is Far from Over." *New York Times*, April 2, 1989. http://www.nytimes.com/1989/04/02/arts/art-view-the-messy-saga-of-tilted-arc-is-far-from-over.html.

Carr, Mary Margaret. "Acquisition Cost - Installed Art in Architecture Works." General Services Administration, January 5, 2017.

Dixon, Matt. "$750K Sculpture Sickened FBI Workers in Miami." *Politico Florida*, December 2, 2016. https://www.politico.com/states/florida/story/2016/12/the-750k-sculpture-that-hospitalized-fbi-miami-workers-107768.

"Final Artist's Concept Presentation for 50 UN Plaza." General Services Administration, May 28, 2010. https://foiaonline.regulations.gov/foia/action/public/view/record?objectId=090004d28130785a.

"Final Concept Review - Buster Simpson." General Services Administration, June 15, 2011. https://foiaonline.regulations.gov/foia/action/public/view/record?objectId=090004d28130785a.

"Final Concept Review - Ursula von Rydingsvard." General Services Administration, February 4, 2014. https://foiaonline.regulations.gov/foia/action/public/view/record?objectId=090004d28130785a.

"Final Concept Review - Odili Donald Odita." General Services Administration, June 27, 2013. https://foiaonline.regulations.gov/foia/action/public/view/record?objectId=090004d28130785a.

Getter, Tyler. "Art Inspection Form - Christopher Sproat, Untitled." Fine Arts Program, General Services Administration, September 21, 2016.

Gibson, Jennifer. Letter to Norman Dong. "Removal of Artwork," October 2, 2015. GSA-2016-000160. FOIA Online. https://foiaonline.regulations.gov/foia/action/public/view/record?objectId=090004d280a5e7f6&fromSearch=true.

"Golden Fleece Awards, 1975-1987." Wisconsin Historical Society. Accessed February 7, 2018. http://content.wisconsinhistory.org/cdm/ref/collection/tp/id/70852.

Goodwin, Michael. Letter to Sabina Sims. "Re: Path Forward Regarding Art Sculpture in Miramar," July 30, 2015. https://foiaonline.regulations.gov/foia/action/public/view/record?objectId=090004d280a5e7f6&fromSearch=true.

"GSA Art in Architecture Policies and Procedures." General Services Administration, November 2010. https://www.gsa.gov/cdnstatic/AIA_policies_and_procedures.pdf.

GSA Art in Architecture: Selected Artworks 1997-2008. General Services Administration, 2008. https://www.gsa.gov/real-estate/design-construction/art-in-architecture-fine-arts/art-in-architecture-program/gsa-art-in-architecture-selected-artworks-1997-to-2008.

GSA (General Services Administration). Planar Pavilions, Denver Federal Center, Lakewood, Colorado. General Services Administration, 2016. https://www.youtube.com/watch?v=ykcfSzMV7WQ.

Haley, Richard. Letter to Norman Dong, January 29, 2016. https://foiaonline.regulations.gov/foia/action/public/view/record?objectId=090004d280a5e7f6&fromSearch=true.

"Introductory Panel Meeting - FBI Building, Miramar, Florida." General Services Administration, August 24, 2010. https://foiaonline.regulations.gov/foia/action/public/view/record?objectId=090004d28130785a.

Lewis, Jo Ann. "Showdown on 'Hoe-Down.'" Washington Post. September 26, 1979. https://www.washingtonpost.com/archive/lifestyle/1979/09/26/showdown-on-hoe-down/b69215d6-5a18-42cf-bc62-34d692a90d8a/?utm_term=.e3af30331902.

Michel, Karen. "When Sculpting Cedar, This Artist Is
    Tireless And Unsentimental." *NPR.Org*, April 28,
    2013. https://www.npr.org/2013/04/28/177969148/
    when-sculpting-cedar-this-artist-is-tireless-and-unsentimental.
Miller, M. H. "A Contemporary Art Titan's (Almost) Secret
    Commune." *New York Times*, October 27, 2016, sec. T Magazine.
    https://www.nytimes.com/2016/10/27/t-magazine/art/mark-di-
    suvero-socrates-sculpture-park.html.
Miller, Michael. "The Dog-Killing Woes of Tom Otterness."
    Observer (blog), October 4, 2011. http://observer.com/2011/10/
    the-dog-killing-woes-of-tom-otterness/.
"Minutes for Final Proposal Presentation, Conference Call with Gary
    Simmons." General Services Administration, September 30, 2015.
    https://foiaonline.regulations.gov/foia/action/public/view/record?ob
    jectId=090004d28130785a.
"Minutes for Third Panel Meeting - Calais, Maine Land Port of
    Entry." General Services Administration, July 19, 2007. https://
    foiaonline.regulations.gov/foia/action/public/view/record?objectId
    =090004d28130785a.
Moynihan, Daniel Patrick. "Guiding Principles for Federal
    Architecture," 1962. https://www.gsa.gov/real-estate/design-
    construction/design-excellence/design-excellence-program/
    guiding-principles-for-federal-architecture.
National Foundation on the Arts and the Humanities Act of 1965,
    Pub. L. No. Public Law 89-209, S. 1483 845 (1965). https://www.gpo.
    gov/fdsys/pkg/STATUTE-79/pdf/STATUTE-79-Pg845.pdf.
Resnik, Judith, and Dennis Edward Curtis. *Representing Justice:
    Invention, Controversy, and Rights in City-States and Democratic
    Courtrooms*. New Haven, CT: Yale University Press, 2011.
Serra, Richard, and Clara Weyergraf. *Richard Serra: Interviews, Etc.
    1970-1980*. Yonkers, NY: The Hudson River Museum, 1980.
"Technical Evaluation of Artists - Calais, Maine Land Port of Entry,"
    August 29, 2006. https://foiaonline.regulations.gov/foia/action/
    public/view/record?objectId=090004d28130785a.
"Technical Evaluation of Artists - FBI District Office, Miramar,
    Florida." General Services Administration, April 14, 2011. https://
    foiaonline.regulations.gov/foia/action/public/view/record?objectId
    =090004d28130785a.
Tepper, Steven J. "Unfamiliar Objects in Familiar Spaces: The Public
    Response to Art-in-Architecture." In *Center for Arts and Cultural
    Policy Studies, Princeton University*, 1999. https://www.issuelab.

org/resource/unfamiliar-objects-in-familiar-spaces-the-public-response-to-art-in-architecture.html.

"Thanks from the Saved Ones." GSA Fine Arts Collection. Accessed February 9, 2018. https://www.gsa.gov/fine-arts#/artwork/26063.

Visual Artists Rights Act of 1990, Pub. L. No. 101–650, 17 U.S. Code § 106A (1990).

"Where's the Art?" General Services Administration. Accessed February 9, 2018. https://www.gsa.gov/real-estate/gsa-properties/visiting-public-buildings/gsa-headquarters-building/whats-inside/wheres-the-art.

CHAPTER 3: THE NATIONAL ENDOWMENT FOR THE ARTS

"29 Pieces, Dallas, TX." NEA Online Grant Search. Accessed February 12, 2018. https://apps.nea.gov/GrantSearch/.

"2017: WALLS." San Francisco Mime Troupe - America's Theater of Political Comedy. Accessed February 9, 2018. http://www.sfmt.org/company/archives/walls/2017.php.

Andrews, Travis M. "Behind the Right's Loathing of the NEA: Two 'Despicable' Exhibits Almost 30 Years Ago." *Washington Post.* March 20, 2017, sec. Morning Mix. https://www.washingtonpost.com/news/morning-mix/wp/2017/03/20/behind-the-loathing-of-the-national-endowment-for-the-arts-a-pair-of-despicable-exhibits-almost-30-years-ago/.

"ART WORKS Guidelines: We Fund/We Do Not Fund." National Endowment for the Arts. Accessed February 12, 2018. https://www.arts.gov/grants-organizations/art-works/we-fund-we-do-not-fund.

"Arts and Artifacts Indemnity Program." National Endowment for the Arts, June 2017. https://www.arts.gov/artistic-fields/museums/arts-and-artifacts-indemnity-program-international-indemnity.

Auclair, Liz Stark. "Art Out Loud: Public Art Takes Over DC." *NEA Arts Magazine*, 2010. https://www.arts.gov/NEARTS/2010v2-arts-capital/art-out-loud.

Batts, Lisa Boykin. "NEA Support Boosted Whirligig Park." *Wilson Times.* March 30, 2017. http://www.wilsontimes.com/stories/nea-support-boosted-whirligig-park,82953.

Bauerlein, Mark, ed. *National Endowment for the Arts: A History, 1965-2008.* Washington, DC: National Endowment for the Arts, 2009.

Binkiewicz, Donna M. *Federalizing the Muse: United States Arts Policy and the National Endowment for the Arts, 1965-1980.* Chapel Hill: University of North Carolina Press, 2004.

Ellison, Garret. "Inherently Controversial: How Grand Rapids Got a Calder Sculpture in the First Place." MLive.com, October 6, 2013. http://www.mlive.com/news/grand-rapids/index.ssf/2013/10/artprize_2013_is_hardly_calder.html.

Fleming, Ronald Lee. "Public Art for the Public." *The Public Interest*, March 2005. http://www.nationalaffairs.com/storage/app/uploads/public/58e/1a5/093/58e1a509377f7647325678.pdf.

"Funders." New England Foundation for the Arts. Accessed February 12, 2018. https://www.nefa.org/about_us/funders.

"H. Rept. 104-170 - Arts, Humanities, and Museum Services Amendments of 1995." Legislation. Washington, DC: United States House of Representatives, June 29, 1995. https://www.congress.gov/congressional-report/104th-congress/house-report/170/1.

Kourlas, Gia. "But Is It Art? In the Case of 'Doggie Hamlet,' Yes." *New York Times*, April 7, 2017. https://www.nytimes.com/2017/04/07/arts/dance/but-is-it-art-in-the-case-of-doggie-hamlet-yes.html?mtrref=undefined&gwh=9653829FD2F24EBC73BBE90B765E3645&gwt=pay.

Loiko, Patricia. Email to Joseph Studemeyer. "Recently Indemnified Exhibition Information Request," September 25, 2017.

"Lyndon B. Johnson: Remarks at the Signing of the Arts and Humanities Bill." The American Presidency Project. Accessed February 12, 2018. http://www.presidency.ucsb.edu/ws/?pid=27279.

Manabat, Bryan. "Arts Council Not Eligible for NEA Funds until 2018." *Marianas Variety*, April 15, 2016. http://www.mvariety.com/cnmi/cnmi-news/local/85407-arts-council-not-eligible-for-nea-funds-until-2018.

"New US Embassy in Islamabad to Get $400,000 Camel Sculpture." The Express Tribune, March 31, 2014. https://tribune.com.pk/story/689550/new-us-embassy-in-islamabad-to-get-400000-camel-sculpture/.

Serrano, Andres. "Protecting Freedom of Expression, from Piss Christ to Charlie Hebdo." Creative Time Reports, January 30, 2015. http://creativetime.org/reports/2015/01/30/free-speech-piss-christ-charlie-hebdo-andres-serrano/.

"Vollis Simpson Whirligig Park (Wilson)." Accessed February 15, 2018. https://www.tripadvisor.com/Attraction_Review-g49674-d8698153-Reviews-Vollis_Simpson_Whirligig_Park-Wilson_North_Carolina.html.

"Walters Presents A Feast for the Senses: Art and Experience in

Medieval Europe." The Walters Art Museum, October 6, 2016. https://thewalters.org/news/releases/article.aspx?e_id=517.

Index